Praise for *How the Future Works: The 7 Steps to Getting There*

We have arrived at a moment where we can backslide into the status quo or transform society for generations to come. *How the Future Works* makes the latter possible -- providing us with a blueprint to deeply consider the future of work. It is a must-read for today's leaders.

Indra Nooyi, former CEO, PepsiCo and author of *My Life in Full*

We know flexibility is the future of work—the big question is how it's going to work. This book combines the latest data with actionable advice on giving people more freedom without settling for less excellence."

Adam Grant, #1 New York Times bestselling author of *Think Again* **and host of the TED podcast WorkLife**

How the Future Works uncovers the key principles for building a culture that connects, supports and inspires every employee in this new all–digital, work-from-anywhere world. It's an essential guidebook for transforming the way people work and unlocking their potential.

Marc Benioff, Chair and Co–CEO, Salesforce

I pay attention to the Future Forum. And if you're interested in folks who take in gobs of data, listen, ask useful questions, and make helpful judgements on how we might work now, you might too.

Priya Parker, author of *The Art of Gathering: How We Meet and Why It Matters*

CEOs confront few topics as complex, urgent, and strategically important as the future of work in a post-pandemic, increasingly digitized world. Brian, Sheela, and Helen highlight pitfalls, provide insight and practical advice to help guide leaders through these choices, and put us on a path to improve work for the benefit of our people and our organizations.

Rich Lesser, Global Chair, Boston Consulting Group

The disruption to work ushered in the era for flexible work forcefully. This insightful book provides a framework with examples for successfully implementing flexible, diverse, and inclusive cultures.

Tsedal Neeley, Professor, Harvard Business School and author of *Remote Work Revolution* and co-author of *The Digital Mindset*.

At a time when the fundamental nature of how and where we work is changing, organizations of all sizes need guidance on navigating what has become a brave new world of work. *How the Future Works* artfully weaves together research, principles and storytelling to help leaders unlock the power of flexible work.

Arvind Krishna, Chairman and CEO of IBM

How the Future Works is as valuable as it is much needed for today's executive. The book is excellently conceived, organized and written. Plus, with the checklist at each chapter's end and the tool kit at the book's closing, it's very easy to turn this into an action plan. Bravo!

Alan Murray, CEO, FORTUNE

How the Future Works is an incredible resource for business leaders as we navigate seismic changes in today's workplace. The founders of the Future Forum are helping to answer some of the bigger questions we're facing as we reimagine work and create new ways of working that can better serve both employees and employers.

Tracy Layney, Senior Vice President and Chief Human Resources Officer, Levi Strauss & Co.

How the Future Works builds a very strong business case to reset how we think about flexibility, resulting in a better, more sustainable work model for both employees and organizations. It provides practical guidance and resources to think through where, when, and how work gets done – and most importantly, why flexibility makes strategic sense. An excellent read for leaders who are re-imagining the future of work post-pandemic, amidst a very competitive talent marketplace.

Helena Gottschling, Chief Human Resource Officer, Royal Bank of Canada

HOW THE FUTURE WORKS

LEADING **FLEXIBLE TEAMS** TO DO THE **BEST WORK** OF THEIR LIVES

BRIAN ELLIOTT
SHEELA SUBRAMANIAN
HELEN KUPP

Published by John Wiley & Sons, Inc., Hoboken, New Jersey.
Published simultaneously in Canada.

For general information on our other products and services or for technical support, please contact our Customer Care Department within the United States at (800) 762-2974, outside the United States at (317) 572-3993 or fax (317) 572-4002.

Wiley publishes in a variety of print and electronic formats and by print-on-demand. Some material included with standard print versions of this book may not be included in e-books or in print-on-demand. If this book refers to media such as a CD or DVD that is not included in the version you purchased, you may download this material at http://booksupport.wiley.com. For more information about Wiley products, visit www.wiley.com.

Library of Congress Cataloging-in-Publication Data

Names: Elliott, Brian (Executive), author. | Subramanian, Sheela, author. |
   Kupp, Helen, author. | John Wiley & Sons, publisher.
Title: How the future works : leading flexible teams to do the best work of
   their lives / Brian Elliott, Sheela Subramanian, and Helen Kupp,
   founders of Future Forum.
Description: Hoboken, New Jersey : Wiley, [2022]
Identifiers: LCCN 2021062493 (print) | LCCN 2021062494 (ebook) | ISBN
   9781119870951 (cloth) | ISBN 9781119871194 (adobe pdf) | ISBN
   9781119871576 (epub)
Subjects: LCSH: Teams in the workplace—Management. | Leadership. | Work
   environment. | Work—Forecasting.
Classification: LCC HD66 .E424 2022 (print) | LCC HD66 (ebook) | DDC
   658.4/022—dc23/eng/20220302
LC record available at https://lccn.loc.gov/2021062493
LC ebook record available at https://lccn.loc.gov/2021062494

Cover Design: Wiley
Cover Image: © Cathal Stadler/Getty Images; Wanlee Prachyapanaprai/Getty Images; elenabs/Getty Images

SKY10033261_032122

Contents

Foreword

In March of 2021, about a year into the pandemic, Slack's executive team was dialed into our regular weekly staff meeting. We were 45 minutes into what was becoming a very frustrating conversation about office reopenings, remote work policies, time zone guidelines for hiring plans, regional compensation adjustments, and a host of other topics that are by now quite familiar to company leaders in nearly every industry.

We were talking past each other, seemingly disagreeing about the most basic aspects of the future we imagined, until our Chief People Officer, Nadia Rawlinson, stopped the conversation: "Hold on: when you ask 'what's going to be different?' are you talking about different from February 2020? Or different from today? It matters because the answers take you in opposite directions."

She was right. Human brains love shortcuts, and it is much easier to imagine the future as just like the past, except for one small difference. For every "we'll go into the office two days each week," there's an implicit assumption: ". . . but otherwise things will be more or less the same as February 2020." But that assumption is wrong, not least of all because it presupposes every employee lives within commuting distance of an office. The world has already moved on.

When you think about the future of work as evolving from our present "normal," things look quite a bit better. Starting from the baseline of the surprisingly impressive performance we've seen with nearly every office worker working from home, we get two new, big advantages. The first, as the pandemic subsides and we learn to better negotiate the ongoing risks and trade-offs, will be a fuller return of the amenities of regular life. More travel, more togetherness, and less risk to our physical health will mean better mental health and happier lives for all.

The second advantage will be the return of in-person communication and collaboration as one of the tools available for us to get work done. This will help in forming relationships, building trust, and approaching certain kinds of creative work. Even after the pent-up demand for seeing colleagues in person subsides, regular time spent together face-to-face will play a key role in the experience of most knowledge workers, including most of those who otherwise prefer to work remotely 100% of the time.

Nadia's question shifted the conversation into the kind of engaged debate that was more characteristic of our normal discussions. In subsequent conversations with dozens of customers, along with fellow software CEOs and industry observers, I've noticed increasing receptivity to an optimistic and open-minded approach to the future of work.

The pandemic highlighted the fact that most organizations had already switched from a mode of operation where digital technologies supplemented in-person communication, to a world where in-person supplements the digital. Now we just need to get our mindsets caught up to that Digital-First reality.

The opportunity we have today is enormous. No adage has proven itself more true in my career than "never waste a crisis," and no crisis has been bigger than this. This is a chance to reimagine how work gets done, to break bad old habits, and make work better for people and companies.

Like the scientists say, you can't unscramble an egg. We need to start thinking about the future we want, given where we are today. We need to avoid falling back to assumptions about a familiar remembered past that is not coming back. My hope is that more leaders will think about this time—and the unforeseeable set of circumstances—as an invitation to get creative, to experiment, to invent, and to take advantage of what will surely be the biggest single opportunity we'll have in our lifetimes to make fundamental changes to how we work. And helping leaders navigate the way forward was one of the reasons I was excited to help launch Future Forum, a consortium backed by Slack.

We all know that work can be more fulfilling, less stressful, more pleasant, and more productive. The purpose of this book is to help you make that happen.

— *Stewart Butterfield, co-founder*
and CEO of Slack

Introduction: The 9-To-5 Just Doesn't Work for Us Anymore (And Maybe Never Did)

When Slack, the enterprise messaging platform, was founded, co-founder and CEO Stewart Butterfield lived in Vancouver, and the company's other founders were located in New York and San Francisco. Together they built a product that enables distributed work among distributed teams, but even still the company's primary headquarters was established in San Francisco. Because, of course it was. "If you want to do inter-bank finance, you have to go to London. If you want to start a giant media company, you have to be in New York. If you want to do movie production, you have to be in Los Angeles," Butterfield told an interviewer way back in 2018.[1] If you want to start a tech company, you have to be in the San Francisco Bay Area, or so the thinking went at the time, at Slack and so many other companies. Indeed, it wasn't long before Butterfield moved to San Francisco himself, so he could be closer to the heart of both the company and the entire tech world.

Despite the fact that the Slack product was designed to allow people to work collaboratively in a virtual forum, at the end of 2019, just before the COVID-19 pandemic hit, the vast majority of the company's engineering staff—79%—were located in the San Francisco Bay area, with only 2% working remotely. The organization wasn't against flexible work per se. There were those high-performers who, once they'd applied, were granted permission to work that way, and occasionally they would hire someone from outside the area. But, as co-founder and Chief Technology Officer Cal Henderson admits, "I was definitely skeptical of it." At the time it was important to company leaders that they have a cohesive group of people located in the same place and coming into the office on a set schedule so they could collaborate and do innovative work.

But that way of thinking caused some challenges. It made hiring more difficult. With rare exceptions, people had to live near Slack offices or be willing to move, despite the high cost of local real estate. When employees wanted to move away, typically for family reasons or to pursue a better quality of life in less expensive locales, the company often lost talented people. "We tried to accommodate really exceptional people when there was no other alternative, but we also let some exceptional people go," Butterfield recalls.

That's essentially where the company was at when the pandemic hit, offices closed basically overnight, and everyone was forced into a kind of grand experiment. Just like we have seen with company after company, in industry after industry, the nature of work changed.

In the beginning, the focus of Slack's leaders was simply on productivity, on how people could continue to achieve pre-set goals in these altered circumstances. They paid close attention to the metrics as things unfolded, and to everyone's surprise, they quickly found that overall, output, quality, and reliability remained strong. "It was surprising how well we continued to operate," Henderson says. Even still, there were some significant variations across teams depending on their circumstances. Parents with young kids, those dealing with health challenges in the family, or those with poor work setups and internet connections struggled more, for obvious reasons. But as the company got better at identifying where problems existed and what those problems were, they were able to provide help—giving people support, space, even equipment—and the outlook continued to improve.

In the beginning, most companies—most people, in fact—thought the shift would be temporary, but as lockdowns were extended, most workers began settling into a rhythm—and not just at Slack, but at numerous companies we worked with during the period. They also made some discoveries about the conventional wisdom that had previously dictated so much of how we worked—and, oftentimes, that "wisdom" just didn't hold up. Because so much of how people were used to working was based on the idea of being present together in space and time, there was an assumption that these things were necessary for collaboration and innovation. Many had relied on whiteboards for brainstorming sessions, for example, but when forced to find another way, solutions—often simple ones—presented themselves. Team members at Slack began brainstorming in an online document where everyone, in their own time, could offer ideas and opinions, and then the group would get together for short discussions once everyone had weighed in. It worked better than expected, as did numerous adjustments to fundamental work habits and processes, like meetings, team building, measurements, and more (all of which we'll talk about in this book).

During that unprecedented time, companies were looking closely at the impact of what was happening, measuring not just productivity, but employee sentiment and engagement to see if business would simply fall off a cliff. But the opposite happened: these new, more flexible work practices were shown to actually *increase productivity*. According to an analysis by Goldman Sachs Group, productivity—defined as the measure of goods or services produced per hour by workers—rose 3.1% during the first year of the crisis.[2]

Within a few months, leaders at Slack had already begun talking about permanently applying some of the changes that had taken place and lessons that had been learned. "It was just very compelling evidence," Butterfield explains. "It was an accident of history that we got pushed into this, but there's been a benefit to forcing this change because there otherwise would have been no way to convince anyone that it would work. I can't imagine how we ever would have come to believe this empirical fact that we could work so well with everyone working flexibly unless it actually happened."

The evidence was convincing enough that Slack's leaders decided to change course. "At some point it felt like we had been operating this way for long enough that we could be confident we would continue to be able to operate this way in the future," Henderson says. In 2020, Slack announced their intention to move forward, not try to go back to how things had once been, by introducing their new flexible work strategy. They opened up hiring within the US and allowed people to keep their jobs if they moved. They began developing tools and methods for people to connect and collaborate from wherever they were and whenever worked best for them and their team. Once they started down this path, it would be hard to go back, but Butterfield's confidence showed in his own choices: He realized he, too, could move away from the Bay Area he had once gravitated to and go somewhere else, which he did when he moved to Colorado. "I realized I can just go," he says, "and it's not really going to make any difference to my ability to lead or do my work."

It's been more than a transition for the company, it's been a transformation that's had a wide-ranging impact, one that we'll continue to talk about through the course of this book. But just in terms of the distribution of talent, by the end of 2021, only 36% of Slack's engineering team was located in San Francisco and the number of team members working remotely on a permanent basis grew from just 2% pre-pandemic to nearly 50%.

One of the main reasons Slack decided to make the fundamental shift to a more flexible way of working is the impact it has on recruiting and retaining employees—the battle for talent—which is one of the biggest challenges that employers of knowledge workers face today. A 2021 joint survey of CEOs by *Fortune* and Deloitte found that 73% said that a *labor shortage* was their biggest external concern, and 57% said that *attracting and recruiting talent* is among their biggest challenges; followed by 51% who said *retaining it* is highest on their list.[3]

As you will see over the course of this book, flexible work offers a real opportunity, not just to attract and retain talent, but to transform the way people work and unlock their potential. One of the reasons that's possible is because so much of the way we had been working pre-pandemic was rooted in old norms and organizational models whose evolution largely stalled out decades ago even as technologies continued to change and workforces became more diverse. It just took a crisis to open our eyes to it and force us to do something about it. As Butterfield put it, "This is no time for retreat to the comfort of well-worn habits. We can't respond reflexively. This moment demands a thoughtful and intentional response and will reward creativity in attempts to build a better workplace and world." And that's far more attainable than some leaders may realize.

Flexible work "has opened up to question every aspect of the work experience; it all needs to be unpacked. The corporate office was the yardstick. It was facetime, it was your calendar, but even before COVID, that wasn't sustainable. We need to think about the employee experience. This is an opportunity to get the most out of your people as a company."

— *Atif Rafiq, President, Commercial and Growth, MGM Resorts International*[4]

Why the 9-to-5 Mentality Needs to Go

The old adage that "time is money" goes way back. It's typically credited to Benjamin Franklin, and it describes the long held belief that more time spent working equals more success. And that may have been true at one time, for some anyway. In the agricultural era, more time in the fields meant more crops getting planted or harvested (of course, that only worked for the owner of those crops or those being paid by the hour or bushel to work the fields, rather than slave labor or indentured servants). Even still, much agricultural work was unlikely to continue after sundown and it's often seasonal, unlike what took root during the Industrial Revolution when a large part of the labor force moved from field to factory to work on a set daily schedule.

As journalist Celeste Headlee, author of *Do Nothing: How to Break Away from Overworking, Overdoing, and Underliving*, put it: "Before the industrial age, time was measured in days or seasons. However, when workers began punching in and out of work, our understanding of time changed, as did our enjoyment of our time off." If people got time off at all, that is. Shifts in factories and mills could sometimes last for ten, twelve, even fourteen hours a day, leaving little time to do much else but eat, sleep, and get ready for another day of work (a notion that may not seem all that unfamiliar to many working today).

Labor movements grew in power in reaction to strenuous conditions, but it was more than just workers who saw the need for change. In the 1920s, automobile titan Henry Ford found business reasons to impose limits on working hours. As someone who kept a close eye on efficiency, he noticed that when employees worked too many hours, they made mistakes and productivity suffered. As a result, he imposed restrictions: eight-hour days, five days a week. He wasn't the first to do this, but he deserves credit for bringing attention to the concept. "We know from our experience in changing from six to five days and back again that we can get at least as great production in five days as we can in six," he said. "Just as the eight-hour day opened our way to prosperity, so the five-day week will open our way to a still greater prosperity."[5] Still, it wasn't until the next decade, in 1938, that President Franklin D. Roosevelt signed the Fair Labor Standards Act limiting working hours for all workers.[6]

It was during that Industrial Era that the concept of work became so tied to measures of time and output, to the point where they were seemingly inseparable. Management practices followed suit, with leaders relying on things like punch cards and monitoring practices to make sure workers were putting in their time and churning out product.

Many of these ideas persisted even as work changed considerably. In the mid-twentieth century, many workers moved again, this time from the factory to the office, but, like the field or factory, there was still a central location where work had to get done—that's where the files and equipment (typewriters, switchboards, fax machines) that enabled work were located, as well as the people you needed to collaborate with to get your work done.

Even today, most of us still think of the workday as some variation of 9-to-5 and the workweek as Monday through Friday. Bosses often expect to see their employees in the office at a certain hour and take note of when they leave (pre-pandemic, at least). This has largely remained true even though, thanks to a slew of new technological tools, the kind of knowledge work that drives much of today's economy doesn't need to be done from anywhere in particular, or during any particular hours. Many of us no longer have to show up in the field where the crops are in order to do our work, or in the factory to assemble widgets, or in an office to connect with colleagues and clients. In fact, the idea that we would wait until we get into the office at 9:00 a.m., or have a hard stop when we leave at night, went away quite some time ago for most of us (if we ever experienced it at all), when our laptops and smartphones started allowing us to carry work home with us in our bags or pockets. 9-to-5 is a concept that just doesn't resonate with most knowledge workers today.

It seems that so much of how we work has changed over the past few decades, and yet so much hasn't. Concepts like presenteeism, clock-watching, and employee monitoring are all still widely practiced in companies across industries, and rarely have we stopped to wonder whether these old habits and expectations still make sense. (Spoiler alert: they don't, as you'll see throughout this book.) Then along came COVID-19, which shut down offices across the globe, and suddenly we couldn't avoid it any longer: We had to take a closer look at the way we work and ask whether it was possible to do things differently—and maybe even in a better way.

As anthropologist, James Suzman, wrote in his exploration of how the concept of "work" has evolved throughout the ages: "By recognizing that many of the core assumptions that underwrite our economic institutions are an artifact of the agricultural revolution, amplified by our migration into cities, frees us to imagine a whole range of new, more sustainable possible futures for ourselves, and rise to the challenge of harnessing our restless energy, purposefulness, and creativity to shaping our destiny."[7]

In other words, if the way we work is rooted in old norms, what's stopping us from changing, and from doing things in a new and better way?

"I see the 40-hour office workweek—an artifact of factory work—finally becoming a thing of the past. Employees will escape grueling commutes and gain more control over their day."
— *Drew Houston, co-founder and CEO of Dropbox*[8]

What Is Future Forum, Anyway?

Future Forum was born because we saw this huge opportunity to redesign work—something that hasn't happened since the Industrial era. We want to help leaders understand that opportunity—which is about far more than just designating some work-from-home days—and all it can do for their businesses.

Future Forum grew out of the fact that Slack has always had a strong research team dedicated to understanding how people work and what can help them perform even better, because the answers to those questions are fundamental to the products the company makes. It has been clear from that research that many workplace practices, structures, and measurements of success haven't kept pace with the massive change we have seen in the last decades in the kind of work people do in the knowledge economy, and how they get it done. Though much of the research once focused on making Slack products work better, there had long been rumblings, led by Butterfield, about starting a "Center for the Future of Work" in order to look more broadly at how "work" as an idea was changing—and more importantly, how it needed to change even further.

But the idea never really took hold, that is until 2020 when so much of the world shut down, businesses had to close their doors, and Slack, like practically everyone else, was forced to do things differently. We suddenly found ourselves in conversations with companies around the globe about how to continue to work under massive new constraints. In the beginning, the nature of those discussions were highly practical: How are you handling this? Are your people able to work like this? What's getting in their way? How are you supporting them? What's working? What are you saying to Wall Street about what's happening?

After a few months, however, things began to settle and executives moved from a crisis mentality to a more philosophical one. We started having conversations with leaders in all kinds of business, and not just tech companies, about how surprisingly well certain things were going, how productivity seemed to be holding steady, if not improving, and how certain people even seemed to be happier and more engaged than ever before, while others were struggling under tremendous challenges. Admittedly, it came as a surprise to many leaders that just because people were largely on their own, working outside the office and, to a great extent, on their own schedules and terms, didn't make them worse employees. With this new realization, gradually the conversations moved from "How do we make this work?" to something else: "Does this work so well that we should be rethinking the way we work, not just for now, but for the long term?"

Out of that context, Future Forum was born, a consortium focused on redesigning work for all types of people. We guide executives to build workplaces that are flexible, inclusive, connected, and ultimately more effective for the world we're living in today. We conduct original research and engage thousands of executives from a wide variety of industries in order to learn from one another, experiment with new concepts, and ultimately push our thinking about what the future can hold.

The upsides of flexible work have been a welcome surprise, of course, but it hasn't all been a rosy picture—and our research has looked at that, too. It quickly became clear that we have created an inequitable system where benefits are not distributed evenly across the board. There was massive unemployment in some sectors, for example, especially where it wasn't possible to shift to different ways of working. And for those working from home, caregiving responsibilities paired with school closures often made work more difficult, if not impossible. These inequities have disproportionately affected women, especially women of color, but flexible work has provided an upside for many historically disadvantaged groups as well. Women and people of color are among the groups who say they want flexibility the most, for reasons we will discuss in later chapters. In fact, now that so many have experienced what flexible work can do for them, the vast majority of knowledge workers say they want more of it. Our research shows that flexibility is the most important driver of job satisfaction behind compensation.

One of the core goals of Future Forum is to understand what people need, to do their best work, and find ways that leaders can meet them where they are so organizations *and* people can find greater success together.

> "To me, flexible work is the future. If there's one silver lining of the pandemic, it's that this time away from the office has allowed us all to reevaluate our priorities."
>
> — *Ben Chestnut, co-founder and CEO, Mailchimp*[9]

Seven Steps to the Future of Work

The need for this book arose out of the work that Future Forum has been doing since its founding. It draws on the experiences of a wide variety of companies—including IBM, the Royal Bank of Canada, Levi Strauss & Co., Atlassian, Dell, Genentech, Salesforce, Boston Consulting Group, and of course, Slack—as well as experts in the field to not just redesign the future of work, but provide a blueprint to get there. Because, without a doubt, the old way wasn't working as well as it could.

While flexibility is not a panacea for all workplace issues, it is a major step in the right direction, if done right. Of course, doing it right can be tricky when companies have been working in a specific way for decades and don't know how to make the shift—because if you want to be successful, it's not a simple retrofit process, where you take old ways of working and move them into a virtual forum. This book aims to help you redesign how you work by taking you through seven key steps, filled with case studies and hands-on advice, to make it happen. After all, there is a real battle for talent going on, and flexibility is what people want. As you will see in the next chapter, it's also what companies in a fast-changing marketplace are going to need if they want to stay competitive.

Why Flexible Work Works

"The workplace will now be wherever work happens, and the workweek will be whenever work happens best for each person."[1] That was how Dropbox CEO, Drew Houston, described the company's flexible work strategy, announced in October 2020, which was a clear break from how they'd worked in the past. Dropbox had largely been an office-centric culture, and they'd invested a lot in creating what Chief People Officer, Melanie Collins, describes as "the most delightful work environment we possibly could." Their office spaces, which are located around the globe from San Francisco to Sydney, Australia, included things like state-of-the-art gyms and world-renowned cafeterias featuring their own signature roasted coffee blend. Office space was such a big part of their culture that pre-pandemic only three percent of its people didn't work out of one. When the COVID-19 pandemic hit and those offices had to close, the vast majority of Dropbox employees were displaced.

Much like what happened at Slack, as the pandemic forced them to pivot, Dropbox leaders were surprised to find that productivity and performance didn't really miss a beat. That caused them to rethink what they'd been doing and accelerated their conversation around the merits and possibilities of flexible work. The pandemic forced more flexibility on companies, of course, but the question for Dropbox quickly became: How could it work over the long-term? What would a flexible work strategy look like if it were dictated, not by circumstances, but by design?

The answer wasn't obvious. Dropbox began by forming a team, co-led by Collins and Alastair Simpson, their Vice President of Design, with representatives from different parts of the company—design, tech, HR—to really study the issue. They took their time and kept an open mind as they looked internally at how their people were responding, as well as externally to benchmark dozens of companies. "We considered everything on the spectrum from full-time to no-time at the office," Collins explains.

Among the models they rejected was the typical hybrid one—where some people work remotely and others continue to come to the office as usual. This is, perhaps, the model most people think of first, but Dropbox decided it wasn't right for them—the main reason being, as Collins explained, because it "creates two very different employee experiences that could result in issues with inclusion, or disparities with respect to performance or career trajectory depending on whether you are in the office or remote."

Instead the team came up with a strategy that makes flexible work the primary experience for all employees. But when the concept was proposed to their leadership team, it was far from an immediate win. There were questions and pushback. Houston, in particular, wanted more detail. It sounded good in theory, but he wanted to be able to picture what a "day in the life" would look like for employees.

As we mentioned earlier, Houston now describes the workplace as being "wherever work happens," and the workweek as "whenever work happens." So, how do you balance those notions with the very real need for team members to connect and collaborate with one another? Instead of the traditional 9-to-5 expectations, the team asked what people really needed to collaborate effectively with one another while balancing individual needs for focus time. The flexible work proposal included the concept of "core collaboration hours"—four-hour windows of time each day when employees would be accessible to one another to do these very things, leaving the rest of their schedule open to get individual, focused work done when it suited them (see Figure 1). That concept raised concerns, like: "How will I be able to meet with people in different timezones?" and "How will I condense eight hours of meetings into just four?"

The team had to come up with answers. Core collaboration hours needed to be aligned to time zones, for example: a window of 9:00 a.m. to 1:00 p.m. on the West Coast synched with noon to 4:00 p.m. on the East

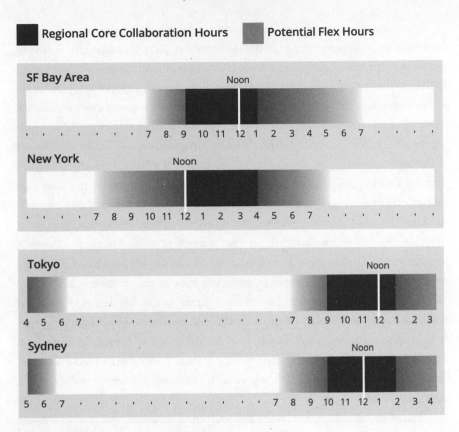

Figure 1 Dropbox's core collaboration hours

Dropbox set "core collaboration hours," or four-hour windows for synchronous collaboration, aligned to time zones versus anchoring to physical locations. The example above highlights collaboration hours for their Americas-based and Asia–Pacific-based teams.

Source: Dropbox

Coast, which meant that everyone could collaborate during a reasonable timeframe but still allowed flexibility in the schedule so people could have lunch with a family member or pick up a kid from soccer practice.

As they sorted through these kinds of issues, it became clear that to be successful, the company needed more than just a policy statement; they needed to create what Collins describes as a "deliberate shift in culture." This meant everything from changing ideas about what should actually merit a meeting (more on this tricky subject later on) to how to offer perks that weren't focused on in-office cafes and gyms.

To introduce the concept and market the change required to support it, Dropbox provided everyone with a dedicated toolkit, an open and evolving guide with practical exercises and advice to help teams focus on the behavior shifts needed to be successful. Topics range from task prioritization to team leadership, and the toolkit focuses heavily on embracing asynchronous work since that's a concept that's been difficult for people to wrap their heads around. Vice President of Design, Alastair Simpson, says, "The two behavior shifts we're focused on the most are getting rid of unnecessary meetings and embracing asynchronous work. We believe implementing these two things makes the biggest difference for our employees based on our research to date." Even as they focused on flexibility, Dropbox knew that in-person interaction was still important, so they adopted plans for their Dropbox Studios—collaborative spaces that employees can use for in-person meetings, team events, learning experiences, or whatever else meets their needs.

Some of the advantages of the new strategy quickly became clear. As we mentioned in the last chapter, flexibility is increasingly something that employees value and look for. It was no different at Dropbox. Based on internal surveys, they found that 88% of their people preferred increased flexibility and 84% stated that they were *as productive* or *more productive* while working flexibly.

But the benefits went well beyond that. Leaders wanted to ensure their new flexible work model was helping them meet their key goals and financial objectives—and early results were more than promising. After implementing the new approach, they saw the following:

- Three times the number of applicants
- 15% faster time to hire
- 16% increase in diverse candidates

That's just one example of how flexible work can work. And not just for tech companies like Dropbox either, as you will see in the coming chapters. Flexible work has huge potential for new companies and long-standing ones, centralized organizations and ones that are globally dispersed, for all sizes and most industries. When done right it has clear benefits for both people and the companies they work for.

What We Mean by Flexible Work

Hybrid, remote, virtual, distributed ... these are all terms you will hear associated with the concept of flexible work, and they all describe work models that differ from the traditional setup that has been the default way in which so many people have worked for decades. For the purposes of this book, we lump them all together under the umbrella heading of "flexible work" (but with an important caveat that we'll get to in a moment).

That's because "flexible work" has a somewhat flexible definition. It encompasses a wide range of options that can be tailored to meet the needs of your company, or even the needs of different teams within your company. And yet far too often people define it far too narrowly. They think only of those employees who sometimes or always work from home (WFH) even though that's just one, rather narrow definition (and, as you will come to learn, typically not the most beneficial one). Flexible work, in our view, is more of a mindset than a specific set of rules or policies. It's about freeing oneself from the outdated notion that work = office and the workweek = 9-to-5. Instead we can push the boundaries of how we think about the ways in which we can work together and offer people more freedom and autonomy to get things done in ways that suit them better. We can choose to focus on which model is going to drive the best outcomes for our business, rather than on where and when that work takes place. This requires some flexible thinking.

For example, the reason why WFH is generally not the most beneficial version of flexible work is because the *when* is actually more important than the *where*. You see, most of the time when people talk about flexibility, they talk about location—and, in fact, most of the common terms we just mentioned, like *remote* and *distributed*, largely suggest this kind of flexibility. But **schedule flexibility** is actually far more important. A Future Forum survey of more than 10,000 knowledge workers across six countries found that 76% want flexibility in *where* they work. That's a significant number, one worth paying attention to, but, perhaps surprisingly, it's not even the kind of flexibility that workers want most. A whopping ninety-three percent of workers said they want flexibility in *when* they work (see Figure 2).[2]

76%
Want flexibility in **where they work**

93%
Want flexibility in **when they work**

Figure 2

Source: Future Forum Pulse, 2021

As you make your way through this book, we invite you to keep an open mind about what flexible work can mean because we have found that those statistics defy expectations for a lot of leaders. Even the most innovative companies, the ones that embrace location flexibility, have struggled with the concept of schedule flexibility. But let's face it: a calendar full of back-to-back meetings from 9:00 a.m. to 5:00 p.m., even when done via Zoom from a home office, is not real flexibility, and it's not what workers are asking for. They want the ability to coordinate schedules with their partners and kids. They want to be able to take time out of their day to rest, workout, or go to an appointment. They want to be able to work on a schedule that allows them to be the most productive. They want the freedom and autonomy to make their lives work and do good work all at the same time.

The numbers also show that the desire for flexibility defies stereotype. It's not just something for younger employees or working moms. The desire crosses age, gender, race, and geographical categories. Even among executives, who expressed a preference for office work, a majority still valued their schedule flexibility.

Because the vast majority of workers are asking for it might be reason enough to consider changing how you work, but it's hardly the only reason. When done right, flexible work offers numerous benefits that can give your organization a real competitive edge.

The Competitive Advantage

It's clear that workers want flexibility, especially schedule flexibility, but that alone isn't enough to convince some leaders to make what can (and should) be a substantial structural and cultural shift. The most convincing reason is the rewards. Mounting evidence shows that flexible work enables organizations to do three key things that are critical across industries:

1) Win the Battle for Talent

As we mentioned in the last chapter, in 2021 the top concerns for CEOs centered on people. As the authors of a Fortune/Deloitte CEO survey put it: "When asked about the biggest challenge they face today, CEOs named one above all others: talent, in nearly every form. Attracting, hiring, retaining, developing, growing, and engaging talent."[3] In fact, winning the battle for talent may be the most common reason companies adopt flexible work programs. As Helena Gottschling, Chief HR Officer for the Royal Bank of Canada, put it when talking about their flexible work model (something we'll look at more closely in the next chapter), "If done right, we believe it could be a true differentiator."

First, let's look at how it can help with an organization's **recruiting** efforts. There's really no way around it: When employees work in an office, they must live within a commutable distance from that office. This limits the talent pool that organizations can draw from. It's also one of the main reasons that companies locate their offices in dense (and often expensive) urban markets, where there are more potential employees to choose from. But flexible work allows you to simply choose the best person for the job regardless of location. It opens up possibilities for both employees and companies. Tracy Layney, Chief Human Resources Officer at Levi Strauss & Co., is located in the Bay Area, but the vast majority of her leadership team is not—a situation she's quite happy with. "I just want the best talent," she told us. "There's all this amazing talent in the world, so why would I want to narrow my choices to people who already live here or are willing to move to a place with a super high cost of living?"

There's also the fact that more people are looking for flexibility, so it's a real draw for companies, and it's an area where they can see an immediate impact. Soon after instituting their flexible work model, Dropbox began receiving three times the number of job applicants that they had gotten previously. We have seen similar benefits at Slack: a 70% increase in job applicants in Product, Design and Engineering after the company allowed for location flexibility.

Because people are looking for flexibility, particularly schedule flexibility, it's a model for **retaining** talent as well. In fact, flexibility ranks second only to compensation in determining job satisfaction.[4] That's because it provides real benefits to workers on a personal level. Research shows that flexible work leads to markedly less stress (six times less with schedule flexibility), a better work-life balance (45% higher), and better overall satisfaction at work (30% higher). And schedule flexibility can be a lifeline for those juggling responsibilities outside of work. The tug of caregiving responsibilities impacts three out of four workers, according to a Harvard Business School study.[5] Those responsibilities can impact job performance and even force some people out the door. But flexible work options can be a game-changer for caregivers. Women with kids, for example, say that the number-one benefit of a flexible schedule is "being better able to take care of personal or family obligations during the day." (Men with kids rate "better work-life balance" as the key benefit.)[6]

Flexibility gives individuals room to meet both their personal and professional obligations. That's important because, as all leaders know, replacing employees is a time-consuming and costly endeavor, one that can amount to as much as twice an employee's annual salary.[7]

2) Engage Employees

Every year Gallup conducts their State of the Global Workplace report, and every year it points to the same problem: a majority of employees are either *not engaged* or *actively disengaged* at work. It's an area where most companies are continually looking to improve because disengagement is expensive.[8] But there is something that has been shown to have a positive impact: flexible work. Before the pandemic employees with at least some flexibility had the highest levels of engagement according to Gallup. That percentage actually rose to its highest point in 2020,[9] despite all the disruptions that the pandemic brought, and the flexible work models that were imposed on companies were likely a big part of that.

One of the ways in which flexibility engages people is through **inclusion**, by making it easier for all kinds of people to participate and feel valued. Flexible work has the advantage of benefiting and supporting those who are commonly left out or sidelined in traditional work structures, which includes groups who have been historically discriminated against (as we'll outline in greater detail later in the book). Flexibility also benefits others who don't fit well into typical corporate structures. For example, Helen finds that flexible work better suits her introverted personality. Remote workers and those in satellite offices are more examples of groups that have traditionally been left behind. Their inability to participate fully in team events or meetings have left many feeling like second-class citizens. But when your meeting takes place in a digital space, everyone has an equal opportunity to participate. These are just a few examples, but there are many more ways in which individual employees can get left out, not because of the quality of their work or ideas, but because of things that should be far less important—like what they look like, how loudly they speak, or where they're located. Flexible work allows companies to intentionally design formats for collaborating, creating, and innovating that are a better fit for all their people.

Flexible work can also lead to better **creativity and innovation**, even though leaders often express concerns that it will inhibit these things that are so crucial to growth. Future Forum research shows this concern is a myth, and in fact where people work has little bearing on how creative their team is (more on this in Step 5). To give one example, there's a persistent myth that the best method is to gather people in a room and brainstorm your way to new ideas. Companies have been doing this for decades, but countless studies have shown that this approach is a waste of time, at best; at worst it can lead to the dreaded groupthink and even harm productivity.[10]

3) Build Better Results

Because it has a positive effect on common business challenges, like recruiting and retention; because it leads to happier, less stressed, and more engaged employees; because of these things and more, flexible work, when done right, quite simply drives better business results.

And yet leaders regularly have concerns. One of the most common ones is that flexible work will negatively impact **productivity**. Some version of the following question comes up often: "If my team members aren't in the office, how will I know that they're working?" The question itself is problematic because it calls to mind the kind of outdated, Industrial-Era mindset, focused on monitoring and presenteeism, that we discussed in the last chapter. We'll talk more about what *is* effective in Step 7, but what's important to know now is that the concern isn't backed up by data. In fact, research shows just the opposite: *flexible work actually increases productivity.*

And, it's important to note, while location flexibility is beneficial, schedule flexibility yields even better results: a more than 30% increase in reported productivity.[11]

One example of productivity gains can be seen in Professor Prithwiraj Choudhury's study of the US Patent and Trademark Office (USPTO) as they made the switch to a more flexible work model. He and his colleagues found a 4.4% boost in individual productivity in terms of the organization's key metric for success—the number of patents examined each month. Contrary to expectations, quality of work didn't suffer with the switch, but employee engagement rose considerably. In 2013, a year after the new policy took effect, USPTO topped the list of Best Places to Work in the Federal Government.[12]

Customer engagement can be positively impacted as well. At Slack, team members found that connecting remotely made it easier to meet with more customers during the day, as well as get time on an executive's calendar since videoconferencing often felt less formal than an in-person meet. Where they used to be able to visit one client a day, sales staff say they can now do three videoconferences in a day. Salesforce found similar benefits: Their Zoom customer calls had 25% higher C-level attendance and their sales teams reported getting back two weeks of selling time due to their virtual sales kickoff taking up less time on their calendars than previous in-person ones.

Another way that flexibility builds better results is by enabling **diversity**, which, as is now well-known, has a positive impact on results. There are numerous studies that support this, including one done by Boston Consulting Group in 2017 that linked diversity and profitability: Companies with above-average diversity among their executive teams saw EBIT (Earnings Before Interest and Taxes) margins that were *9 percentage points higher* than those who were below average. Even more striking, those same companies reported innovation revenue that was *19 percentage points higher* than that of companies with below-average leadership diversity—45% of total revenue versus just 26%.[13] Diverse companies also tend to grow faster, be more innovative and adaptable, have higher cash flow, and even be better at building leaders.[14]

In spite of the great potential of diverse organizations, especially in solving today's most complex problems, many leaders struggle with the friction that comes with diverse teams. Flexible work, while not a total solution, is a tool that can help for a variety of reasons. For one, about 60% of the Black labor force in the US is located in the Southeast, compared to only one-third of private sector jobs.[15] Location flexibility allows companies to attract employees who live far from their offices. We have already seen how this benefited Dropbox, who saw a 16% increase in diverse candidates. As a result of the transition to flexible work, Slack has hired one-third more remote-based historically discriminated employees than office-based.

Future Forum research shows that large majorities of Black, Hispanic, and Asian respondents in the US all want flexible work—which means it can have a positive impact on recruiting and retention among these groups. The same is true for women, and we have already talked about some of the benefits to working moms and other caregivers who are disproportionately female. Flexible work can also offer a better experience to groups that have been historically discriminated against. For example, Black employees who work remotely have a higher sense of belonging than those who work in the office.[16] There are likely a variety of reasons for this. As Stanford professor, Brian Lowery, explains, office-centric work can perpetuate outsider status: "Black employees can experience stress associated with working in a predominantly white workplace, which contributes to a lower sense of belonging. Importantly, it might not be work activities per se driving these effects, but all of the big and small social interactions that make up much of our work days."[17]

Finally, it's worth noting the impact flexible work can have on your **bottom line**. Retaining employees saves companies money. Increasing productivity makes companies more money. Decreasing the need for costly expenditures on things like office buildings in expensive urban centers and travel to and from different client and company locales frees up resources that can be put to better use elsewhere—on those things that will drive the outcomes you want. Think of it this way: Would you rather invest money in the seats your employees occupy or in the things that will enable those employees to do their best work, no matter where they sit?

What's Getting in the Way

Given all the potential benefits to flexible work, one has to ask: Why isn't everyone doing this?

At a Glance: The Benefits of Flexible Work

Flexible work helps companies **win the battle for talent**, **engage employees**, and **build better results** by having a proven positive impact in the areas of:

Recruiting	Innovation
Retention	Customer Engagement
Productivity	Diversity
Creativity	Your Bottom Line

One answer is that status quo bias is real, and our default instinct is often to return to old ways of doing things because that's what we know and that's what we're comfortable with.[18] After all, that was what got us and our organizations here in the first place. If it was good enough then, why isn't it good enough now? Slack CEO Stewart Butterfield talks about this resistance to change in terms of meetings. Despite the fact that just about every executive he's ever talked to about the subject believes their organization has too many meetings and could gain a lot by being more efficient about how they are structured and run, "They literally do nothing to try to make the improvements because it's not what they're used to and they don't have good ideas about how to get it done." It's an issue we're tackling at Slack because too many meetings inhibits schedule flexibility, which is central to how we want to work and something we all need to get a lot better at managing.

Another answer is that flexible work models haven't always been successful. While the pandemic accelerated the need for and the adoption of flexible work options, various versions of it existed long before. Pre-pandemic there were a number of high-profile companies that tried it, only to reverse course when a new CEO came on board or they didn't see the results they were looking for. But many of those early attempts failed before new technologies changed the landscape of what's possible. The availability of broadband connection, SaaS tools, and the consumerization of IT have made things possible that simply weren't before, and the pandemic sped up advancements even further.

One of the biggest reasons why flexible work hasn't always worked in the past, and can still fail today, is because companies don't always get it right. They often fail on two fronts:

- The What: Too many people don't fully understand what flexible work could or should mean for them, particularly the crucial importance of schedule flexibility.

- The How: Too many people don't understand how to execute it successfully.

This book is going to show you how to do both....

The What: Digital-First

As noted above, there are different versions of flexible work, and different companies have given different names to their flexible work strategies, as you'll see throughout this book. But there is a version of flexible work that we advocate based on our research and experience: **Digital-First**. It is the backbone of flexible work, and you need to adopt a Digital-First approach in order for flexible work to really work.

What do we mean by Digital-First? Let's start by defining what it isn't:

- Digital-First is not the office-centric way of the past.
- Digital-First is not just about location flexibility.
- Digital-First is not a mandate about how many days a week people can work from home.
- Digital-First does not mean never in person, or that all work gets done remotely.

Digital-First means making the switch from a mode of operations where digital technologies supplemented in-person communication as a way of getting work done, to one where in-person supplements the digital in order to build a more connected and inclusive way of working for everyone. This requires a switch in mindset. Companies can still have a headquarters, but it's going to primarily be a digital HQ, supplemented by physical office space. Companies can still build a connected and collaborative culture, but it's going to be built largely in digital forums, supplemented by in-person connections. And perhaps most importantly, Digital-First means embracing and prioritizing a truly flexible way of working, one in which people are given the freedom of choice—in terms of both when they work and where they work—in order to unlock their potential and enable them to perform at their best.

That desire for flexibility in *when* people work, as well as *where*, is one of the reasons we think terms like "hybrid" or "remote-first" aren't the right fit—they focus on location. To enable real flexibility, companies need to adopt a Digital-First mindset, recognizing that the only way to give people the schedule flexibility they need is to leverage digital tools that allow them freedom, not just in where they work, but when.

Moving to a Digital-First approach means putting as much thought and effort into the digital infrastructure that supports productivity and collaboration as we once did into our office buildings, desk configurations, conference rooms, and floor plans. Making this change is about more than just a switch in emphasis: Like anything else, if not executed well—if you don't get the how part right—you won't be successful.

Digital-First: *n.*

A flexible work model that requires companies to make a switch, from a mode of operations where digital technologies supplemented in-person communication as a way of getting work done, to one where in-person supplements the digital, in order to build a more connected and inclusive way of working for everyone. Digital-First means embracing a truly flexible way of working, one in which people are given the freedom of choice—in terms of both when and where they work—in order to unlock their potential and enable their best performance.

The How: Flexibility within a Framework

Digital-First does mean giving your people the freedom and autonomy to do their best work from a place and on a schedule that best suits their needs, but the idea of employee freedom can scare off some leaders. That is, until they understand that flexible work isn't about total freedom or unstructured chaos. That's not something employers would be willing to give, but it's also not what workers are really asking for. While most don't want to be in the office from 9:00 a.m. to 5:00 p.m. (or worse, 8:00 a.m. to 8:00 p.m.) five days a week, they still want some structure in their workday. In fact, nearly two-thirds (65.6%) said they want a balance between full flexibility and a predictable framework.

What businesses need in order to be successful is to create what we call *flexibility within a framework* to support their Digital-First work model. They don't realize that for flexible work to really work, it requires much more than just a policy statement. It requires a significant change in your company culture, processes, and infrastructure. Too often companies miss the bigger picture and the larger opportunity.

That could have been true for Dropbox. Their leadership team was on board with the concept of location flexibility in the beginning, but there was hesitation about schedule flexibility and what that would mean in terms of collaboration among their people. The pandemic forced them to experiment, and the company found something that worked. (They call theirs "virtual first," but it's a good example of a Digital-First strategy.) Then they created a framework of policies, tools, and infrastructure to support it.

Dropbox took a big bet on something that was untested and unfamiliar to them. It required significant changes and investment, but the improvements they've seen in recruitment, onboarding, and diversity speak for themselves. And that's just the beginning for them. As they continue to experiment and adjust to what works, they are sure to see more of the benefits that flexible work can bring, providing them with a real competitive advantage.

This is where the next part of this book comes in. You don't have to take a big bet on something that's completely untested. Through Future Forum's original research and work with companies that are paving the way, we have distilled what companies need to do to make the switch to Digital-First into seven key steps that will get you there. They will help you reimagine how the future works, and then design a framework that supports your new vision and drives results. It's not a quick-and-easy process, but as you saw with Dropbox—and as you will see with the many other company examples in this book—it's well worth it.

How the Future Works: The 7 Steps to Getting There

Step 1: Stand for Something: Agree on Purpose and Principles

Helena Gottschling had been working at the same organization for more than three decades when they decided to make the fundamental shift toward flexible work. Gottschling is the Chief Human Resources Officer for the Royal Bank of Canada (RBC), an institution with a long history dating back to 1864. It has more than 86,000 employees worldwide serving an excess of 16 million clients.

It was feedback from employees that first caused RBC to consider this shift. During the pandemic, when so many people were working remotely, they did a series of surveys, focus groups, and town halls across the globe, out of which came a clear message: The vast majority of their employees appreciated the personal benefits of flexible work. That dovetailed with the main business purpose for RBC, which was to gain a competitive advantage in the battle for talent. "We're in a very competitive marketplace for talent," Gottschling says. "If done right, we believe flexibility could be a true differentiator."

RBC's "Enterprise Principles" for Flexible Work

1) **Flexible work is here to stay**: Hybrid work arrangements will be supported where feasible and optimal for the business, clients, and employees.
2) **Our approach starts with our business strategy**: Platforms have the flexibility to adopt a tailored approach to optimize across teams, roles, and regions, while enterprise standards set the parameters to enable consistency and scale.
3) **Proximity still matters**: Being close to our colleagues and the communities we serve is core to our culture and will remain so in the future; for the majority, this means residing within a commutable distance to the office.
4) **Strategic investment is required**: To fully enable our employees, we will invest in technology, infrastructure, and skills to operate in a more flexible environment.
5) **Inclusive culture with growth opportunities**: Employees should have a consistent and meaningful employee experience with access to development opportunities regardless of work arrangement or location.

Flexible work options, while available, were not widely used across RBC before the pandemic, so what they were contemplating was a real sea change for the company. One of their first steps was to create what they called their "enterprise principles." This was particularly important because of the global diversity of the company: RBC is a complex organization with multiple lines of business spanning 36 countries. They needed principles to help guide the right decisions and drive behavior change across the organization. "The nature of the work across our various businesses is very different, so we knew out of the gate that we couldn't push out a one-size-fits-all solution," Gottschling explains. Someone working in personal banking, for example, might have to be on hand to meet with customers, whereas someone working in analytics or accounting would have very different requirements. Their principles—five in all—set a foundation, helping to create alignment across the large, diverse, and geographically dispersed organization and guide leaders in determining what's best for their respective businesses.

Getting to a place where they could distill their own vision of flexibility into five simple, easy-to-understand principles that applied to the entire organization was a process—one that involved lots of discussion about how to tailor some of the best practices of flexible work to the specific needs of their business. For example, when RBC launched their flexible work strategy, they focused on both schedule flexibility and location flexibility, but with some boundaries. They decided that, for their organization, "Proximity still matters" (Enterprise Principle number three). That doesn't mean employees have to be in the office five days a week, but similar to how "Digital-First does not mean never in person" at Slack, RBC's leadership recognized the importance of bringing people together every now and then in intentional ways (something we'll discuss in greater detail in Step 5). "Proximity still matters" communicates to the organization that it's important to RBC that people are generally located close enough that showing up once a week—or maybe a week at the beginning or end of each quarter, depending on what works for their team—is an option for meetings, events, or simply to plan and connect with colleagues.

"What we didn't want," Gottschling says, "is to have one group say that all their team members could move to a different region and never come into the office while another group that does similar work says the complete opposite." You'll note that "Proximity still matters" doesn't dictate that people need to live in a certain region or city. Instead, Gottschling points back to employees to make the decision by asking "What's your tolerance for commuting?" based on the team's frequency of in-person gatherings. You can see how this specific principle helps to provide a balance between flexibility and structure—something that both leaders and employees say they want.

Early feedback on their flexible work strategy has been positive, and the company has been using it in recruiting materials, like their "Why RBC?" aimed at potential new employees. There are some skeptics in their ranks, but when doubts arise Gottschling likes to remind people that they worked remotely for at least 18 months during the pandemic and they didn't skip a beat. That doesn't mean there isn't more work to be done to ensure their strategy is successful.

"We're going to learn as we go, keep having conversations about what works and what doesn't, and we're going to get better at it," Gottschling says. They will make adjustments along the way, but she believes flexibility is here to stay. And she's leading by example: "I will never, personally, go back to five days in the office every week." And, she projects, neither will most of their people.

Just like with RBC, the process of creating your flexible work purpose and principles at the leadership level—which is what you will learn to do in this step—is how you will start to gain the understanding and alignment necessary to drive an organization-wide change in how your people work together.

Your Flexible Work Purpose: What's Your Why?

Flexibility, especially schedule flexibility, will only succeed if you are willing to set aside outdated conceptions of how work should be done and think differently. But with so many different ideas about what flexibility can mean to each person, team, and company, it can be hard to band together and create this kind of shift. You should start by understanding your purpose and aligning leaders around it: WHY do you want to enable flexible work in the first place?

Why start here? Because too many organizations have jumped into defining a flexible work strategy without understanding why they're implementing it, other than the fact that their employees want it or they want to keep up with peer companies who are already doing it. This is a flawed approach for a couple of reasons.

First, as we know from research, companies with a clear purpose have an advantage. Increasingly, employees—especially younger ones—say they want to work for purpose-driven organizations that can clearly articulate how they serve their people, customers, and community. These kinds of companies perform better, too. A global *Harvard Business Review* study found that companies with a clearly articulated purpose had higher growth rates. They were also better able to innovate and transform—capabilities that are crucial in today's competitive marketplace. As one executive in the study put it: "Organizations do better when everyone is rowing in the same direction. A well-integrated, shared purpose casts that direction. Without the shared purpose, organizations tend to run in circles, never making forward progress but always rehashing the same discussions."[1] The same could be said about taking a purpose-driven approach to anything as fundamental to your business as how work should get done.

Second, as we explained in the last chapter, flexible work can mean a variety of things. If you did a Google search in 2021, as companies were figuring out how to move forward after pandemic-imposed restrictions eased, you would have seen everything from "going back to the office full time" (Goldman Sachs) to "working two-to-three days in the office" (many Fortune 500 companies) to "fully remote" (Gitlab) and "virtual first" (Dropbox). You would have found companies that were focusing only on a Work From Home (WFH) policy, and others that were offering not just location flexibility, but the kind of schedule flexibility that a greater number of workers really want and that is inherent in the Digital-First approach that we recommend.

To move forward, your leadership team needs to talk through the real business purpose behind flexible work. After all, this isn't just something you do to make your people happy. It can have a real impact on your bottom line. Purposes may vary somewhat from company to company, but they all generally come back to addressing one key issue: talent. As we touched on in the last chapter, flexible work helps companies attract top talent. It allows them to recruit from a larger pool of candidates. It helps them engage and retain the talent they already have. As you have seen already, RBC's purpose for flexible work was to address the needs of their current employees, who valued flexibility, and to be a differentiator in a highly competitive market-place for talent—which is compatible with their overall business purpose of "helping clients thrive and communities prosper." There may be additional, often secondary, reasons for a flexible approach—like allowing more agility and connection among a global workforce or an initial savings on real estate costs—but your main Flexible Work Purpose will almost surely center on your people.

At Slack we touched on similar themes when defining our purpose. After much (often messy) debate over the course of several months, we articulated our purpose through a set of key questions and beliefs that the leadership team needed to agree on:

- **Do we want access to the best, most diverse talent pool that exists?** There's a giant pool of talent that today is inaccessible to us because unless someone lives within commuting distances of our offices, we didn't hire them.

- **Will employees continue to demand flexibility as a basic benefit?** In the same way compensation is market driven, work-from-home policies, flexible schedule policies, and a Digital-First approach *are going to be expectations that employees demand.*

- **Do we want the agility that comes with being Digital-First?** The ability to collaborate across cities and suburbs, time zones, and around the globe; the removal of the barriers of "remote offices" being second class; and the speed that comes with shared knowledge and understanding of goals all are better served by a Digital-First model over office-centric.

It's in those often messy debates about how flexible work will support your business objectives that you begin to build alignment among your leadership team. You will then continue to build it as you take that purpose and translate it into a set of core principles that will help you to introduce your flexible work strategy and align the rest of your organization around it.

Flexible Work Purpose: *n.*

A statement explaining the main business purpose behind your flexible work strategy. It should clearly articulate *why* flexibility is important to your company and be compatible with your organization's overall purpose and values.

Flexible Work Principles: *n.*

Similar to company values, principles are core beliefs and values that support the organization's flexible work purpose. They are not specific mandates or specific rules, but guidance to help communicate how you expect people to behave, how they can make decisions that align with your intentions, and generally bring your *why* to life.

Your Flexible Work Principles: How Can You Support Your Purpose?

Principles don't look too different from core company values in some ways. They're not focused on the tactical how (like how many days you should be coming into the office), but more on the mindset required to make a significant shift in how you do business.

You already saw RBC's principles, which cover:

- Their overarching intention: "Flexible work is here to stay."
- How they're approaching the shift: "Starts with our business strategy."
- Three main things they care about when considering what flexibility means to them, and how they want flexible work to play out in their organization: "Proximity still matters," "Strategic investment is required," and "Inclusive culture with growth opportunities."

Principles are meant to be shared across an organization in order to provide direction, consistency, and inspiration as people make the big changes required to enable flexible work. Think back to the example of RBC: The bank has multiple business units across numerous countries. They have a wide variety of functions and tens of thousands of employees, all with unique needs. How do you create a flexible work strategy that can accommodate all that?

The answer is that you "don't push out a one-size-fits-all solution," as Gottschling put it. Instead you allow for flexibility in the execution of your strategy, and you enable individual department and team leaders to decide what works best for their group—but within a framework and with top-level guidance. Your principles act as a kind of North Star. Any decision that gets made at any level—about how often a team will meet, for example, or how to measure team or individual success—should be consistent with those principles.

Principles are also meant to help people begin to think in new ways. You have to always remember that flexibility upends traditional ideas about how work is supposed to be done, ones that date back far longer than the careers of anyone reading this book. Redesigning work and replacing old notions with something new and better will take time and reinforcement. It's another reason why spending the time up front to create clear and considered principles is so important. They provide your people with that North Star, that anchor, as they go about changing not just how they do their work, but how they think about it as well.

Some principles will be unique to your business, like RBC's "Proximity still matters." Contrast that to the many companies that have gone in the opposite direction by instituting "work from anywhere" policies that allow employees to relocate to an island in the South Pacific if that's what they choose. Open source software company Gitlab, for example, is fully remote with no corporate headquarters at all, so they would have different requirements.[2] Your principles should marry your flexible work strategy with the overall needs and objectives of your business.

That said, we have found that many principles are pretty universal across different organizations and industries. (See the sidebar for some examples.) One is to "Ensure equitable access." This is such an important one that we devote the next step to it. What's key to know now is that flexible work is meant to enable your people to do their best work. You undercut that if people feel like they lose access to knowledge within the company, opportunities for advancement, or a sense of community and camaraderie with coworkers if they don't show their faces in the office. It's not enough to simply say, "You can work from home if you want to." You have to make sure that working from home doesn't make people feel like second-class citizens.

Examples of Flexible Work Principles

Following are a few more examples of principles that executives from a variety of companies are using to reshape the way they work:

- **Provide flexibility and freedom for people to do their best work.** Think beyond people's ability to WFH a few days to what it means to provide flexibility in *when* as well as *where*, and measure performance in terms of *outcomes* not *activity*.
- **Give team-level autonomy to achieve goals rather than top-down directions.** One size almost never fits all. Provide global guidelines for work arrangements and let teams decide on specifics to suit their needs.
- **Ensure equitable access to opportunity.** Design your working norms to ensure equity in access to opportunity, regardless of your work arrangement, for diverse talent and those in what were once "remote" offices. Use this as an opportunity for leaders to find new ways to help people build their networks and create opportunity from anywhere.
- **Maintain a learning mindset by being adaptive.** Prioritize and create opportunities for experimentation and sharing best practices. Norms and practices will need to continue to evolve as we learn. Commit to measuring outcomes and adjusting as you go.

We're going to talk more about how you can start the process of defining and aligning around your flexible work purpose and principles in the next section. But before we do that, there are a couple of useful hints to keep in mind when articulating your principles:

- **Provide context:** Your principles should help your people envision what flexible work will look like and understand what matters most when putting it into practice.

- **Keep it simple:** Don't overengineer this. RBC has five principles. Most companies have between three and six. It's up to each business to decide what's most important to communicate, but the more complicated you make it, the harder it will be for your people to appreciate your vision.

You'll find further guidance on how to create your purpose and principles in the toolkit at the back of this book (see "A Simple Framework for Creating Your Flexible Work Purpose and Principles" on page 180).

The Process: How Leaders Can Start to Create Alignment

Even something that sounds straightforward, like defining your purpose or principles, can be a messy endeavor when you start talking about it among different people with differing opinions—as anyone who has ever tried it will know. We've been through a flexible work transformation at Slack, and we have worked with numerous companies as they've done the same, so we know what it's like. From those experiences we've distilled some best practices that will make your discussions a little less messy, providing focus and structure as you start defining and aligning around a purpose and principles that will guide this fundamental shift and continue to drive the change going forward.

The following sections will walk you through **six ways to start creating leadership alignment around flexible work**:

1. Start with the right orientation
2. Check your assumptions
3. Dedicate resources
4. Involve your people early
5. Lead with transparency
6. Keep a "more to learn" mindset

Start with the Right Orientation

When you start your conversations to align on a flexible work purpose and principles, keep in mind that organizations that are successful at this have a common orientation. They've made the conscious decision that they're not going back to old ways of working that really don't make a lot of sense anymore. Instead they have stated their intention to move forward with an understanding and appreciation of how much has changed and how it's time that notions of work caught up to those changes.

When defining our flexible work principles at Slack, we began with one that speaks to this very idea: "We aren't going back; we're moving forward, with all that we've learned." That principle grew out of disagreements that took place among our leadership team about how (and if) we should return to the office once pandemic restrictions were lifted. As we debated the topic, some leaders expressed a desire to return to how things were. That was when our then Chief People Officer, Nadia Rawlinson, asked a question that really hit home about whether we wanted to go backward or whether we wanted to move forward.

In our talks there were real questions about whether going back was even possible now that so many people had experienced, and appreciated, a new way of doing things. There was also concern that if we tried to, we'd be missing a real opportunity. As our CEO, Stewart Butterfield, put it: "We had a once in a lifetime opportunity to reinvent the way we worked—for the better." We decided we didn't want to waste the opportunity.

We made that clear to everyone in our company by making it principle number one. When we published our principles, we also expanded on it and included the following context:

> "**We aren't going back; we're moving forward, with all that we've learned**. We've embraced flexibility; we've relocated, we've welcomed unexpected Zoom cameos of kids and pets and gotten to know our colleagues on a more human level. We know that this new way of working **works**, and employees will expect this flexibility going forward."

The Change Must Be Leader Driven

The question of how people will work together is so fundamental to any business that a move toward flexibility must be driven by top leaders— preferably the CEO. In fact, the Boston Consulting Group (BCG) was able to measure the importance of CEO participation in their Future of Work survey. It found that flexible work strategies that were CEO-lead progressed faster than those that weren't (see Figure 1.1).

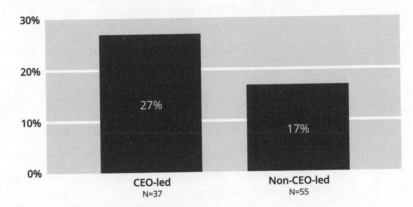

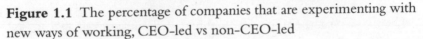

Figure 1.1 The percentage of companies that are experimenting with new ways of working, CEO-led vs non–CEO-led

Source: Boston Consulting Group CEO survey, June 2021. *Options*: Not started, Early Stages, Well Along, Experimenting.

At Slack the change to flexible work started with dedicated time and attention from our CEO and executive team, including weekly dates on the calendar for in-depth conversations. Those conversations largely centered on three main questions that can provide a starting point for any organization:

- What problems are we trying to solve?
- What business outcomes do we want to achieve?
- What perceived challenges are we facing?

The team was largely starting from scratch because much of the research and examples we're including in this book didn't exist yet or hadn't been widely published. It took more than two months of conversations to agree on a purpose and come up with a set of principles that were ready to be shown to the rest of the organization. It may seem like a lot of time spent up front, but it was worth it because of the alignment we were able to build as a result.

Check Your Assumptions

What came out of those executive conversations at Slack—and what we hear over and over again from the organizations we work with—is a common set of concerns among top leaders about how, and even if, flexible work can really work. Following are some of the ones we hear most often:

- How will I know my people are actually working and being productive?
- What will happen to our culture if we aren't in the office?
- Won't it hamper our ability to innovate and be creative?
- Won't new and younger employees be left behind with fewer opportunities for apprenticeship and learning?

When you hear them, or if you think of them yourself, it's a good opportunity to check your instincts and ask why you believe that flexible work will have the kind of negative impact that these questions imply. We have talked already about how many of these concerns aren't rooted in data. Flexible work has been linked to higher productivity, not less, for example, and doesn't negatively impact creativity based on Future Forum research.

Gottschling says she gets asked these kinds of questions at RBC, too, and she has a useful way of addressing them. When she's asked how managers will know if someone's actually working, for example, her typical answer is: "How did you know they were working when they were in the office?" You will know your people are being productive if you set clear goals, check in with them regularly, and pay attention to the results they get. These are things any good manager should be doing no matter where someone works. As Gottschling points out, "Frankly it's no different. It's not like you are looking over their shoulder to see what they are doing on a day-to-day basis in the office either."

In fact, her tactic of answering a question with a question is a useful one for addressing all these concerns:

How will I know my people are working and being productive?
- How did you know they were productive before?

What will happen to our culture if we aren't in the office?
- Why do we need an office to create culture?

Won't it hamper our ability to innovate and be creative?
- Why do we believe the office is required for innovation and creativity?

Won't new and younger employees be left behind with fewer opportunities for apprenticeship and learning?
- Who did office-based learning work for the most, and why do we think it's the best way to learn?

So you don't think we are simply dodging these common questions, we assure you we will address each one in more detail in later chapters. We bring them up here to show the importance of checking your reflexes from the start—to become more conscious of default ways of thinking that may get in your way.

Think Differently

RBC published their "Hybrid Work Playbook for Managers" to help their people make the transition to flexible work. In it they address some common concerns with the following guidance.

You may be tempted to believe employees are less productive and effective outside of the office.
- **Instead try:** Identify the root cause of the problem. If an employee underperforms, it may not only be a location issue. Consider what support you need to provide so they can be successful.

(continued)

> **You may be tempted to** equate face-time, hours worked, and accessibility to productivity.
> - **Instead try:** Foster a trusting culture; focus on impact and desired outcomes that are aligned to business objectives as well as behaviors reflecting the Leadership Model.
>
> **You may be tempted to** feel the need to control and oversee progress.
> - **Instead try:** Empower the team to be their best by providing autonomy and space to do the work.

To put it more broadly, ask yourself why you believe people need a fixed schedule in the first place. Or, why do any of us need to be available eight hours a day for meetings? If your answer is because we've always done it that way, then it really is time to examine your thinking. After all, just because something worked in the past doesn't mean it will work in the future. And it doesn't mean there isn't a better way to do it right now—a way that can lead to even better results.

Dedicate Resources

A fundamental shift like this one isn't going to work if a company simply puts out the purpose and principles and leaves it at that. It will take time, investment, and long-term accountability to make something like this work. It will also require a shift in how you think about allocating some of your resources, so that needs to be part of your leadership discussions.

For example, instead of looking at flexible work as something that will require a big, new investment, think about it more in terms of *reallocating* resources. All that time and money you once put into your real estate portfolio and office layout—figuring out who got what office and which departments went on which floors to enable collaboration—can now be shifted toward determining which digital tools and infrastructure will best enable those collaborations. Investments in many of the perks you once offered to attract top talent—like in-office restaurants and gyms—can be redistributed to individuals to use in ways that will best serve them and their work.

You will also have to rethink some of your people resources. There must be people focused on making flexible work successful, and not just through the transition, but over the long-term as well. At Slack we formed a dedicated "Digital-First task force" composed of senior members across geographies and functions (HR, communications, IT, etc.), as well as core teams that are responsible for the work to move us forward. They worked directly with Slack's executive team for support, feedback, and ultimately, implementation of new policies. Some companies are even creating a new role, a Flexible Work Leader, because like anything in business, if someone isn't accountable, it probably isn't going to work.

Involve Your People Early

A Future Forum survey of remote workers found that more than two-thirds (68%) of executives want to work in the office all or most of the time—that's *three times* the number of non-executives who said the same.[3] Remember, employees have a clear preference for flexibility: 93% want schedule flexibility.

There's obviously a disconnect here between executives and employees. What's driving it? Future Forum's survey looked at that too, and one of the main culprits is the fact that the two groups have very different experiences of work. Executives have a 62% higher rate of satisfaction than employees. They also report a better work–life balance (78% better) and a better ability to manage stress (114% better). These numbers aren't all that surprising when you consider the fact that executives tend to have stronger networks, more autonomy, and better access to resources like space and childcare that support their work. In essence executives have always had more flexibility in their work, so their need for a company-wide policy supporting it is far less.

You won't be able to bridge this disconnect unless you get feedback about your flexible work plans from people at all levels of your business—and you get it early. At Slack we created advisory groups with employees representing different regions, employee resource groups, and functions to get input about different aspects of our strategy or potential points of failure. RBC also made a point of bringing in multiple perspectives. "We often think about our work preferences and the experiences we had growing up in the bank," Gottschling says, "but you really have to think about it through the employee perspective. I often remind leaders that they are simply a focus group of one. What we really have to guard against is projecting our personal preferences into the actions we take."

Lead with Transparency

This guidance goes hand in hand with what we just covered. A flexible work strategy is about enabling your people to do their best work, so your people need to understand it. They need to know your *why*—the purpose behind the changes you're making—as well as what those changes will look like and how they will be impacted. But organizations often miss the mark in creating this kind of transparency. For example, Future Forum's survey revealed another big disconnect within organizations when we asked executives and non-executives about post-pandemic reopening plans. Two-thirds of executives believed they were being transparent about their plans while fewer than half of employees agreed. And employees who don't believe their employers are being transparent report substantially lower job satisfaction, and are far more likely to be open to new opportunities outside their company.

One of the main reasons we started in this first step by asking you to define your flexible work purpose and principles is not just to get alignment among your executive team. It's so you have something to show to your entire organization. It's a way to begin communicating broadly and build greater alignment. It's also a way to open up conversation about your plans. We will come back to the concept of transparency and communication throughout this book because it's crucial to creating change—any change, really, but especially the kind of fundamental, organization-wide change we're talking about here. Transparency is what allows you to build trust with your people, and you're going to need that trust to do something as big and bold as redefining the way you work.

Keep a "More to Learn" Mindset

Finally, you can continue to build trust through transparency by admitting up front that your flexible strategy is a work-in-progress and you don't have all the answers. Starting with those first conversations about your purpose and principles, and continuing as you hone your strategy and put it into practice, your company will be best served by keeping an open mind and a willingness to learn. This is a new way of operating for most companies, so you will need to try things out, pay attention to what works, and be willing to adjust and adapt. Business isn't stagnant, as we all know, and your flexible work strategy should grow and change with the changing needs of your business. As Gottschling said about RBC's plans: "We're going to learn as we go, keep having conversations about what works and what doesn't, and we're going to get better at it."

Checklist for Step 1: Stand for Something

☑ Is your leadership team aligned on the main business purpose behind implementing a flexible work strategy?

☑ Have you translated that purpose into clear and concise flexible work principles to communicate to the rest of your organization?

☑ Have you gotten feedback from all levels of your organization about whether your flexible work principles resonate?

☑ Are you ready to proceed with an open mind and flexible plans as you continue to create and implement this bold new strategy that will fundamentally change the way you work?

Step 2: Level the Playing Field: Create Guardrails for Behavior

Early in her consulting career, Helen worked with a colleague who she describes as an outstanding leader and manager and as someone with the capacity to be competent, engaging, and empathetic all at once in her client interactions. It was a highly effective mix. Even in tough rooms filled with hard-charging executives, she always found ways to win people over.

The catch? She was the only one among her peers with a four-day workweek. She was adamant about spending that extra day off with her kids, and she rarely wavered when pressured by clients, colleagues, or just her heavy workload. Instead she carefully crafted her schedule to make it all work. She didn't shoulder any fewer assignments than her colleagues and her results were just as good, if not better.

Despite her results, this leader's choice of a nontraditional work schedule came at a cost to her career—a "slower slope," as she once described it. She insisted the tradeoff was worth it, but Helen could never reconcile the

47

feeling of unfairness. In the end neither the woman, nor Helen, stayed long at the company. Both moved on to better opportunities.

This isn't an unusual story: historically, employees who have flexible arrangements in terms of when or where they work risk being deemed less committed to the organization or not as much of a team player—despite the value they brought to their companies.[1] This notion is especially challenging when you consider who is most likely to prefer flexibility. In our survey of knowledge workers across the US, 87% of Asian American respondents, as well as 81% of Black and 78% of Hispanic respondents, prefer flexibility, compared to 75% of their white counterparts (see Figure 2.1).

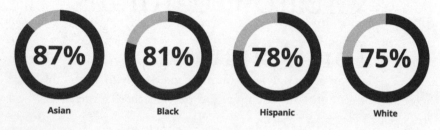

Figure 2.1

Source: Future Forum Pulse, 2021. US-only

There are differences among genders, too. 85% of women want flexibility compared to 79% of men (see Figure 2.2).

Figure 2.2

Source: Future Forum Pulse, 2021. US-only

Working fathers report higher levels of work-life balance (40% higher) and a greater ability to manage work-related stress (61% higher) compared to working mothers.

And it's not just historically-discriminated groups that prefer flexibility in their work. It can be people who don't fit into traditional office cultures, including introverts, or it can be anyone who has ever worked in a satellite office. In 2019, Mike Brevoort, an engineering leader at Slack, made 23 trips between his hometown of Denver, Colorado, and Slack headquarters in San Francisco. No one was requiring Brevoort to fly to San Francisco so often, but he found that if there was a big meeting or executive presentation, he couldn't participate equally if he dialed in. Just about everyone else in those meetings had an office on the executive floor, so he knew they were starting conversations before meetings and continuing them after they ended.

It also just didn't work well to be the only one on screen in a conference room full of people. At the start of a meeting, everyone could see him, but then someone would go to share a document and suddenly his face would be replaced. He described it as being "out of sight, out of mind" because it became difficult to get people's attention or interject with a thought. Then there was the fact that he couldn't read people's facial expressions, hear whispered comments, or banter with colleagues. Brevoort started traveling so often because he knew he had to be there in person to be fully included, and because if he wasn't being seen and heard by the executives in those rooms, he knew it could forestall his career.

It was frustrating (to put it mildly). Frustrating that he had to spend so much time away from his wife and five children. Frustrating that he was losing so much time to the banalities and vagaries of travel. Frustrating that he would barely recover from one trip before he was jumping on a plane for the next. It was tiring and disorienting, and, as it turned out, not entirely necessary—not if the company had just been more intentional about how they enabled flexibility within their organization.

Brevoort first joined Slack when the company acquired his startup. He'd already proven that he could build his own company, so there wasn't much stopping him from doing it again, or from taking his talents elsewhere if his frustrations grew too great. The company stood a real chance of losing him, but the pandemic hit before that could happen and everyone moved to working from home.

Suddenly Brevoort felt like he could get it all done without leaving Denver. When it came to executive meetings or presentations, everyone appeared equally as a face on screen, as they held them via video conference. Most communications outside of meetings—whether about a new product idea or a simple check-in to see how someone was doing—happened in a Slack communications channel. It didn't matter where someone was located because everyone was meeting, coordinating, communicating, and sharing information in the same way, using the same tools. Without his packed travel schedule, Brevoort found that not only was he able to strike a better work-life balance, he was also able to "get more quality work done." He could do all that because he had *real* flexibility now that, as he put it, "Slack is our headquarters."

If companies really want to unlock talent in their organizations, there are much better ways than what the leaders we just described had to go through. And they were leaders, so they had more options in their situations than most employees. In Step 1, we talked about the importance of principles in guiding executive decision-making, but principles set at the executive level are not enough: You also need guardrails to make sure those principles can be translated throughout your organization in ways that are effective and keep the playing field level so you can get the best out of all your people.

What Are Guardrails?

Guardrails are just what they sound like: they're the protective railings that keep you from veering off course. They create the framework in which your flexible work principles can live and thrive by providing a guard against the kind of double standards across employee groups that so many have experienced. They also guard against what we call *faux flexibility*, which describes policies that appear to be flexible, but still don't give people the freedom and autonomy they are asking for and need in order to make their lives better (i.e. you have the flexibility to WFH, but only one day a week and you still need be available from 8:00 a.m. to 5:00 p.m.). Or, the term can describe behaviors that run counter to flexibility (i.e. executives who still come back into the office full-time, five days a week, which can implicitly signal that to *really* succeed, people would need to abandon flexible options).

Think of it this way: If your purpose is to unlock the power of talent in your organization, then guardrails are there to ensure that actually happens. Because if you're not intentional about how you implement flexible work, you could end up having the opposite effect—creating a greater opportunity- and growth-divide between those who choose more flexibility and those who don't, similar to the "slower slope" career that Helen's colleague described. Research from Nicholas Bloom at Stanford in 2014 showed that, in one company, people working from home had lower promotion rates than their in-office counterparts—a full 50% lower—despite being as or more productive.[2] It's not clear from the study if the company was aware of the risk of uneven experiences, or if they did anything to avoid it. But it's still a potential pitfall to be aware of, and one you can actively manage against. We have seen similar issues ourselves, and you probably have too: People who vary from the standard in-office, all-day work arrangement can suffer penalties, often ones they don't deserve. By being intentional about not just what flexible work means to your organization (that purpose and those principles you just created), but *how* you implement it, executives ensure that flexible work models are actually respected and adopted within the organization—and that they have the intended effect of unlocking talent rather than suppressing it. Otherwise you risk creating inequitable access to opportunities, knowledge, and connection for your more distributed or remote employees.

To help you create effective guardrails, we're going to look now at three main areas where they're most needed and talk about the impact they can make on the employee experience. The three types of guardrails that we'll cover are:

1. Leadership guardrails
2. Workplace guardrails
3. Culture guardrails

Guardrails: *n.*

Guardrails are the agreed-upon guidelines or parameters for behavior that will keep your principles in place. They will help people translate your principles into day-to-day habits and practices that support your flexible work strategy.

Leadership Guardrails

Flexible work is like just about anything else that's integral to your company's success: To make it work, leaders have to set the tone from the top. Without leadership modeling the right behaviors, the principles will fail. What follows are ways that leaders can help ensure their organization lives by their flexible work principles.

Lead by Example

An executive in a real estate firm once described to us how, during an important meeting, most participants dialed in, but all the senior executives could clearly be seen on one tile, indicating that they were together in the boardroom. They assumed no one would notice, but everyone did. It sent a signal that the office was where people needed to be, even though that wasn't their intention. The company wanted to promote flexibility, but the behavior of their leaders undermined the concept. This is an example of *failing* to lead by example.

Leading by example is a concept you have surely heard before because it's simply good practice in any circumstance. When it comes to flexible work specifically, leading by example means that if you, as a leader, are still coming into the office on a typical 9-to-5 schedule every day, then you're sabotaging the strategy and undermining its principles (even if you don't mean to). No matter what you say, no matter what your official policy states, if employees see you in the office regularly, they will believe they need to do the same if they want access to growth and opportunities.

At Australia-originated software company, Atlassian, leading by example meant "stricter rules" for the executive team. Chief Operating Officer, Anu Bharadwaj, explains: "Even after it was deemed safe to return to the office, we decided executives would not go in for more than one day each week and would not hold in-person meetings, without our extended teams, more than once a quarter, with the exception of social events." Slack did something similar when adopting what we call our "executive speed limits." CEO, Stewart Butterfield, went around the room and asked each of his direct reports what commitments they would make to set an example. One that emerged was everyone committing to leaders to spending three days a week or fewer in the office. There was further guidance on how that limited time should be spent: on team events and customer interactions. In other words, the office is for those things that really require people to be present. That was the message Butterfield wanted leaders to communicate through their actions.

Take Symbolic Actions

A great way to lead by example is to take symbolic actions. Find ways to highlight flexible work across your organization. They can be simple actions, like when all executive team members at Telstra, Australia's leading telecommunications company, changed their public profile pictures to show them working from home.[3] Or they can send a broader message. At IBM, CEO Arvind Krishna, shared the IBM "Work From Home Pledge" early in the pandemic—not just to the organization, but on social media for all the world to see. The Pledge grew out of the experience an IBM consultant was having as she tried to balance working from home with having a 10-month-old baby who couldn't go to daycare. One day her baby fell just before she had to get on a video call. Her child was okay, but her team could tell she was flustered with everything she had to manage. That got them talking about their new work situation and the new set of needs that came with it. They started challenging the usual norms of doing business and asking questions like, "If we're working from home, do we really have to be camera ready for *every* meeting?"

That conversation resulted in the team coming up with a list of new norms for the work-from-home, lockdown era. (See sidebar on the following page for the list.) They started sharing the list with others, and word about it spread quickly. Within about a week it came to the attention of senior leadership, and that's when Krishna put it out on social media, to signal his support. This was early in the pandemic, when the company was navigating the sudden switch to working remotely for nearly all of their more than 250,000 employees. Since then, IBM has broadened its definition of flexible work to well beyond just working from home, encompassing schedule flexibility and hybrid (sometimes in, sometimes out of office) arrangements. As a result, team members are working on a new pledge to support their new style of work.

Show Vulnerability

That example highlights another way leaders can reinforce their flexible work principles: by showing vulnerability. Change can be uncomfortable, and it can make people feel like they're on shaky ground. In those early

---

The IBM "Work From Home Pledge"

I pledge to be **Family Sensitive**.
I pledge to support **Flexibility for Personal Needs**.
I pledge to support **"Not Camera Ready"** times.
I pledge to **Be Kind**.
I pledge to **Set Boundaries** and **Prevent Video Fatigue**.
I pledge to **Take Care of Myself**.
I pledge to **Frequently Check In** on people.
I pledge to **Be Connected**.

---

days of the pandemic, Chief Human Resources Officer, Nickle LaMoreaux, remembers Krishna saying often to their leadership team: "Remember, every day you are now being invited into somebody's home. It's important to act as guests with the kind of courtesy that's expected from them." It was a great way to frame the sort of attitude leaders can bring to everyday situations to normalize flexibility and help people feel more comfortable with it. You can do this by saying hi to the kid who accidentally interrupts a video call—or, better yet, by bringing your own family on to wave a quick hello. When taking time in your flexible schedule for an exercise class or to see your daughter's school play, let people know not just when you will be unavailable, but why. Spell it out in your status message—*spending time with mom for her birthday!*—or however you communicate with your team.

Slack's then Chief Marketing Officer, Julie Liegl, brought her kids—just eight and five years old—into one of the first company-wide meetings during the pandemic, and the gesture communicated to the more than 2,000 people attending via video conference that she was a real human being who was juggling things too. Feedback was immediately positive. As Senior Customer Success Manager, Christine McHone, said, "When Julie Liegl's daughters climbed on her lap during a company all-hands meeting, it set the tone for the support we'd receive."

Workplace Guardrails

A successful flexible work strategy requires leaders to redesign the role of the workplace. What that looks like exactly will depend on the needs of your organizations, but doing so effectively will require you to be intentional about setting guardrails to keep people from reverting back to old habits. The following are some examples of guardrails that have been effective in helping to set the tone across different kinds of businesses, which will get you thinking about how to set your own.

Shared Space Is for Teamwork First

In our Digital-First culture at Slack, showing up to the office is no longer the default; it's the exception. As our CEO Stewart Butterfield explained, "Getting teams together in person should have a purpose, such as team building, project kick offs and other events that are planned in advance, pairing flexibility with predictability."[4] Being intentional about the role of the office in this way creates a more structured view of what flexible work can be.

We also got rid of the "executive floor." Before moving to a Digital-First strategy, Slack's corporate headquarters in San Francisco had a tenth floor that was tricked out with a large boardroom and executive briefing center and a ninth floor C-suite where the CEO and other executives had offices. If there was an important meeting happening at Slack, it was always on one of those two floors. They were known as the place to hang out to show you were around. To get people to think differently about the use of office space, we dismantled that and don't believe there will ever again be a need for an executive floor. Per our new guardrails, when leaders are in the office, they'll most likely be there to meet with their teams. For other interactions, as Brevoort said, "Slack is our headquarters."

It's likely that you, too, will need to redesign the way you use your office space (a concept we will talk more about in Step 5). Instead of plans for cubicles and corner offices, companies like MillerKnoll have focused on thoughtfully designed social commons that foster collaboration and connection. There may be more emphasis on creating zones for different kinds of work—quiet floors for concentrated work, for example, paired with social floors for team gatherings. If your "workplace" is no longer a building, that opens up a whole range of new possibilities for how you use your physical space.

Keep a Level Playing Field

In order to level the playing field, leaders need to drive a consistent experience and avoid "in-person favoritism." Outside of intentional time together, meetings should be structured to enable remote participants to be equally present and part of the discussion. To ensure that was happening at Slack, we adopted the guardrail of "one dials in, all dial in," meaning that either everyone gets together in a room for a meeting or everyone participates remotely, even if that means logging on to a video conference from a desk in the office.

Guardrails like this one aren't always easy to make work, especially when they go against ingrained habits. It took quite a bit of experimentation and practice to get this right (a process we'll tell you more about in Step 4), and ensure that executives were modeling the behavior. For example, by holding product review meetings where everyone dials in (and, in fact, there's not even a conference room booked), the pressure to come in to "the room where it happens" is lowered, and the playing field is leveled for employees who get the opportunity to present to an executive only a few times in a year.

It's also important to think about the variety of methods you can use to encourage participation. Not everything requires a calendared meeting via video conference, which can disadvantage some groups, like those in different time zones, parents who are wrangling kids, or introverts who are unlikely to speak up on a crowded video chat. Don't get us wrong: video conferencing is a great tool, one that has been a lifeline for so many, but it's not the only tool you have. Sometimes communications platforms, chat, voice, and even asynchronous video—pre-recorded videos that people can watch on their own schedules—can work even better. There are a wide variety of tools out there for things like virtual whiteboarding, asynchronous brainstorming, or collaborating virtually on written documents. Be conscious of which tools you use and don't just default to yet another meeting that crowds people's schedules (more on this later in the step).

"Studies show that many executives are holding on to the remnants of the past and failing to see this as an inflection point in the workforce. If employers don't pay attention and take action to recreate the best of what we've learned working virtually in the office and in hybrid work environments, then opportunities for inequity could skyrocket."

— *Ella Washington, organizational psychologist*
and the founder of Ellavate Solutions;
Georgetown University's McDonough School
of Business[5]

Rethink the Role of Offsites

Instead of just focusing on which days of the week people should come into the office—which is the approach many companies have taken—companies should be thinking about enabling teams to organize regular events that meet their own needs for team-building and productivity. That will likely mean equipping team leaders with new insights and tools to help them do this.

For example, in a flexible model where team members are working from different places and at different times, people need to be given sufficient advance notice of events. Team leaders also need to be intentional about how their offsites are run. Priya Parker writes convincingly on this subject in her book, *The Art of Gathering: How We Meet and Why It Matters*: "Gatherings crackle and flourish when real thought goes into them, when (often invisible) structure is baked into them, and when a host has the curiosity, willingness, and generosity of spirit to try."[6] Leaders can answer four key questions to make sure they are being intentional about making their gatherings effective:

1. How can I be sure attendees will be comfortable and motivated?
2. What's the topic and what do we need to achieve and produce?
3. Who will facilitate the event and how?
4. What tools will we need?

Executives need to think about how they can support team leaders in creating more effective gatherings, ones that are not only productive, but foster a sense of belonging. In the past, many companies have focused on in-office perks like free meals, coffee bars, or massages to do this, but those things won't work for a flexible, distributed team. Instead leaders need to give people better tools for both in-person and digital "offsites," like team-level budgets for events, as well as a menu of options (pre-approved items like food and swag and pre-approved vendors to provide them), they can easily pick from. Leaders also need to provide people to support these kinds of efforts, like facilitators who can help team leaders conceive of and plan the right sort of gatherings to meet their needs.

Culture Guardrails

A flexible work culture is going to be different than an in-office one, naturally. But more than that, creating a new flexible work strategy provides companies with the opportunity to address some challenges that have long been part of traditional workplace cultures. We address three big ones here, but there will likely be more that come up as you tailor your strategy to the needs of your business.

Move beyond Meeting-driven Culture

It's a ubiquitous complaint in corporate culture: practically everyone is overwhelmed by meetings. And there are real questions about whether meetings are necessary to get things done, or if they are getting in our way far too often. In a survey of managers across a wide range of industries, researchers Leslie Perlow, Constance Hadley, and Eunice Eun found that more than 70% of people believed meetings were unproductive and inefficient, and 65% said meetings keep them from completing their work.[7]

It's time to rethink the meeting. At Slack our executives led by example on this by declaring "calendar bankruptcy." They removed all recurring meetings and one-on-ones from their calendars so that they could consider each one and add back only what was truly necessary. In a message sent out to the entire company, the purpose was explained this way:

- "We're in a new distributed world and gotta change the way we work!"
- "There are lots of legacy meetings that have changed owner, purpose, scope—let's start with a blank slate to determine what's *really* important!"

This doesn't mean there were no more meetings. It just means that leaders got a lot more intentional about the time they were taking up on people's calendars. We found that so many meetings could be eliminated or broken up into parts. For example, your monthly sales meeting might start with a status update. Why not send that out beforehand? Presentations can be shared as decks or asynchronous video so people can review them in their own time. Tactics like these can lessen your meeting time considerably, and then time together can be more meaningfully spent on meaty discussions or team building. For this to happen, however, leaders have to be more intentional about meetings and employ some forethought and planning. As Priya Parker wrote in *The Art of the Gathering*, "90% of what makes a gathering successful is put in place beforehand."

Dropbox uses what they call their "3D" model for planning meetings: debate, discuss, decide. We would add a fourth D for "develop"—time spent focused on honing individual skills or other professional development opportunities. If a meeting doesn't achieve at least one of those four objectives, then it doesn't need to be a meeting. (See our "Do We Need a Meeting?" tool in the toolkit at the back of this book for more on this.) Other tools can be used to disseminate information or get a status check, freeing up much more time in your schedule, and the schedules of your team members, to do the kind of work that really moves things forward.

Guardrails can also be put in place to counter the assumption that people need to be available eight hours a day, five days a week for meetings. Tactics that we've seen work include Levi Strauss & Co.'s "No Meetings Fridays," which aims to reduce internal meeting load and provide a day dedicated to focus time. Google adopted "No Meeting Weeks" years ago for some teams, and similarly Salesforce has adopted "Async Weeks" as a way to not only give people a respite, but also get meeting owners to think about whether each meeting is needed or could be cut in terms of frequency, attendance, or both. Slack's Product, Design and Engineering team has "Maker Weeks" and "Maker Hours"—two-hour blocks, three days a week, where people can turn off notifications and do focused work. (This is a great area to make use of some of the experiment-and-learn tactics we'll cover in Step 4 to see what works for your organization.)

Challenge the Role of the Brainstorm

One of the common concerns about flexible work is that it will stifle creativity and innovation. After all, how can we come up with new ideas and solve tricky problems unless we gather together in a room and hash it out on a whiteboard? People often have trouble imagining other ways because they simply haven't tried them. And in fact, there's good evidence to suggest that they should. Numerous studies show that the often lauded brainstorming session is a waste of time, at best; at worst it can lead to the dreaded groupthink and even harm productivity.

So-called "brainwriting" has been shown to be a better way to generate new ideas, and it requires a kind of hybrid approach that flexible work is particularly well suited for. In fact, the best known way for groups of people to generate new ideas is to work individually before working together.

Brainwriting starts with individual work, allowing time and space for people to think deeply and freely about ideas without fear of judgment or the influence of louder or more senior voices in the room. You ask everyone to commit their ideas to paper, and only then are they shared and debated—an approach that has been shown to elicit better results. According to the *Harvard Business Review*: "A meta-analytic review of over 800 teams indicated that individuals are more likely to generate a higher number of original ideas when they don't interact with others." By contrast, the old way of brainstorming "is particularly likely to harm productivity in large teams, when teams are closely supervised, and when performance is oral rather than written."[8,9]

One of the reasons the brainwriting approach works so well is because it gets more people involved. By allowing ideas to be generated ahead of review, you help create psychological safety for diverse teams and involve more voices that might normally go unheard in rooms where senior and more extroverted voices tend to dominate. It also helps guard against remote workers becoming alienated from such processes. Remember that one of the main reasons that Mike Brevoort ended up traveling to headquarters more than 20 times in a year was because he didn't feel like he could fully participate if he dialed in from Denver. He was able to find a solution, albeit a highly imperfect one, in traveling back and forth, but a lot of employees won't have that option or may feel less comfortable contributing ideas in a large meeting or brainstorming format. It's worth thinking about how much insight, creativity, and expertise you are missing out on by making it harder for all people to participate.

Challenge Your Own Thinking

Practically all of us have "grown up" professionally in a 9-to-5 culture, and inherent in that culture are ways of thinking that we may never have examined very closely. Sheela remembers early in her career working until the wee hours of the morning and being lauded for her "selfless" and "relentless" behavior as a result. Some of the most memorable advice she got in business school was to "burn the candle at both ends until you're in your forties and then reacquaint yourself with your friends and family."

"No pain, no gain" had always been Helen's family motto until she ended up burning out while still in her twenties from a job that entailed 100-hour workweeks, frequent travel, and a long commute. During a discussion about work-life balance with a partner in her firm, the woman casually mentioned that her personal goal was to see her kids twice a week—not day, but *week*.

Brian was taught early on that an attitude of "seldom wrong, never in doubt" was key to success, meaning few around him willingly admitted when there were gaps in their knowledge or they didn't have all the answers. This approach proved to be a real liability at his first startup, where there was a whole lot he didn't know—that, in fact, no one knew. He had to get past that ingrained way of thinking fast in order to enlist the help of others in finding solutions to complex issues—otherwise the venture could have failed.

We're hardly anomalies in the corporate world. So many of us have internalized lessons over the years that we've had to unlearn for the sake of our own success as well as that of the businesses we work for. It's time to challenge some of our old notions about what makes someone good at what they do. Like, working more = working better. Or, employees can't be trusted to get stuff done on their own. These are default ways of thinking in most corporate cultures, but what makes us so sure they're right? After all, have we ever really tested them?

In fact, there's lots of evidence to suggest that they aren't right. Evidence showing that stress and burnout make us worse at what we do, not better. That lack of trust demotivates employees rather than motivating them. If we really want to unlock the potential in people, then we need to keep our eyes trained on what really delivers results and stop rewarding behaviors that undermine them. Think about that the next time you praise someone for answering emails late at night or being in the office first thing in the morning before anyone else. Because it's the quality of work and the results it drives that matter most, not when or where you do it.

Why Guardrails Really Matter

Since the adoption of Levi Strauss & Co.'s flexible work strategy, Chief Human Resources Officer, Tracy Layney, goes into the office two-to-three days a week on average, and the week we talked to her was no different. On Tuesday she had a houseguest, so it was helpful to be in the office with fewer distractions. She got up in the morning, did the typical rush-hour commute, and stayed all day. It was like the old days again, except she was mostly by herself, connecting with her geographically dispersed team members remotely. Then, the next day, she took a couple of calls from home in the morning before taking a break to get some exercise. She later drove to the office and resumed work around 11:00 a.m. She stayed into the evening so she could attend a colleague's work anniversary celebration. It was a long day, but one that benefited from off-hour commutes each way. The day after that, she worked from home and knocked off around 3:00 p.m. so she could make her son's cross-country meet.

All three days looked very different in terms of both where she worked and when, and that flexibility allowed her to balance personal needs— for exercise, family connection, less time lost in Bay Area traffic—with professional ones. She still got plenty of work done, but more efficiently and with less stress than if she'd had to compartmentalize her day. Because let's face it: this is just how life is. One day is rarely the same as the next.

There are always personal and professional needs that we have to balance. Flexible work simply allowed Layney to better accommodate that reality.

Some version of this flexibility would benefit so many people. The needs of each individual will be different, of course. Instead of a child, someone might be caring for an elderly parent; instead of getting some exercise, someone might have other physical or mental health needs to attend to. Religious holidays, different geographic locations, and even the fact that some people work more productively at night because they simply aren't morning people—all these things and more, really aren't all that difficult to accommodate if we can allow ourselves to think differently about work. We leave behind, or leave out entirely, so many when we can only imagine one way of working: nine-to-five (or six or eight), five (or more) days a week.

What's more, flexibility disproportionately benefits historically discriminated groups and caregivers—the groups most often left behind at work. Not enabling flexibility is a loss, not just for them, but also for our corporate communities and our bottom lines. Study after study shows that diverse teams outperform their peers. They grow faster, are more innovative, and adapt faster to external and internal events. Flexible work enables this kind of diversity. "I think the greatest opportunity is, of course, pipelines," explained Professor Tsedal Neeley, author of *Remote Work Revolution*. "Pipelines are getting expanded in extraordinary ways. . . . You now can hire people from other parts of the country without asking them to move." Why is that important? It gives you a more diverse talent pool to choose from, and it benefits all types of people, especially underrepresented minorities. As she explained, "You can hire someone without having them extracted from their communities . . . They can stay where they are and work for you, which is hugely important when it comes to retention and job satisfaction."[10] And the tortured efforts many business leaders have had to make in past years to retain key employees can feel unnecessary when you consider them through the lens of flexibility.

Take Harold Jackson, for example. Just about every executive we know has a story about losing a great employee or jumping through hoops to try to keep one because the person needed or wanted more schedule flexibility, location flexibility, or both. Jackson was one such example for Sheela, who interviewed dozens of candidates for the position of head of analyst relations at Slack, none of whom measured up to him. But Jackson lived in Kentucky, where his family lived, so hiring him meant he had to relocate to California.

Initially Jackson came on his own, leaving his family behind and commuting home on weekends. Eventually his family followed, but they didn't stay long. They didn't like the Bay Area and returned to Kentucky. Jackson wanted to move back too, but Sheela admits she was hesitant at first. Slack was only a few years old and was in a stage of high-growth, so her mentality was that work gets done in the office. She agreed to try to work something out for Jackson's sake, but the company didn't have the infrastructure to make it work. She tried and tried to find a solution, during which time Jackson continued to commute back and forth and then eventually moved to New York, where Slack already had an office, so he could at least be in the same time zone as his family. Finally, after more than two years, it finally happened: Jackson got to move home just as the pandemic hit and we all started working flexibly anyway.

Since then, Jackson has been promoted several times and the impact of his work shines through the company. The effort it took to give Harold flexibility was not a good use of time and energy, especially for something we all adjusted to quite quickly when the pandemic forced our hands. A really important thing to understand about the kind of guardrails we've talked about in this chapter is that they're so often things that companies—most of them anyway—have needed to redesign for some time. As Tracy Layney put it, when it comes to flexible work, "there is stuff we have to guard against, like being biased against different groups, certain people not being visible enough, too many meetings, and overloading people until they burn out. There are real things we have to be careful about, but *these things existed anyway*." The shift to flexible work presents an opportunity to address some of these long-standing barriers and drains on productivity in a more comprehensive way.

We will continue with this in Step 3, when we talk about translating your principles and guardrails for ensuring equitable practices into team level norms. The first two steps have been largely about setting the tone from the top in order to create boundaries and expectations for team leaders to follow. Next we will empower teams to create their own practices that best suit their individual flexible work needs.

Checklist for Step 2: Level the Playing Field

☑ Do you understand what guardrails are and why you need them to support flexible work and fulfill its purpose of unlocking potential for *all* the people in your organization?

☑ Have you considered what guardrails you might need to put in place around Leadership to ensure that executives are modeling the behaviors they want to see in others and not undermining the potential for success?

☑ Have you considered what guardrails you might need to put in place around your Workplace to help people reimagine the role of the office and ensure a level playing field in a flexible work environment?

☑ Have you considered what guardrails you might need to put in place around your Culture to challenge old habits and norms and replace them with new, more effective ones—including how you're going to break your meeting-dependent culture?

Step 3: Commit to How You'll Work: Develop Team-Level Agreements

"For all that we've been able to achieve while many of us have been separated, the truth is that there has been something essential missing from this past year: each other. Video conference calling has narrowed the distance between us, to be sure, but there are things it simply cannot replicate."[1]

That was the message from Apple CEO, Tim Cook, in a June 2021 email informing employees of a new policy requiring most of them to return to the office on Mondays, Tuesdays, and Thursdays, with the option of continuing to work remotely the other two. In May of the same year, Google CEO, Sundar Pichai, announced similar plans requiring most employees to work from their offices at least three days a week. Numerous other companies adopted similar plans.

The backlash at Apple was swift. Just two days after Cook's memo, employees responded with one of their own, in which they pointed to a profound disconnect between executives and employees on this subject. In a letter addressed directly to Cook, a group of "remote work advocates" wrote: "We would like to take the opportunity to communicate a growing concern among our colleagues that Apple's remote/location-flexible work policy, and the communication around it, have already forced some of our colleagues to quit. Without the inclusivity that flexibility brings, many of us feel we have to choose between either a combination of our families, our well-being, and being empowered to do our best work, *or* being a part of Apple."[2]

Google and other organizations have met with similar reactions to their top-down policies, and it begs the question: What goals are these policies furthering? If the purpose of flexible work is to engage, retain, and enable talent, then the backlash these companies have faced suggest that their approaches may not be having that effect. These sort of blanket policies leave out an important consideration: What sort of flexible work guidelines will actually *work* for your people?

We believe that the approach these companies took missed the mark on two fronts. First, they are an example of faux flexibility: They have the appearance of flexibility without actually giving employees what they need and want most, which is autonomy and choice. And when it comes to the location flexibility they do offer, they limit choice for reasons that seem more arbitrary than designed to support employees and enable their best work. (Why Mondays, Tuesdays, and Thursdays? Why not Tuesdays, Wednesdays, and alternate Fridays?) Instead of real flexibility, these policies treat everyone as if they have the same needs and requirements to do their best work, which is obviously not the case.

The second issue is that, intentionally or not, these kinds of approaches communicate a real lack of trust in their teams. Arbitrary, top-down rules suggest leaders don't believe that teams can figure out for themselves how to balance what works best for them personally with what will make them most productive professionally. And that lack of trust is more likely to undermine employee engagement than enhance it.

It's probably because of these reasons that some companies have already backtracked. Amazon, which announced it would call staff back to the office three days a week, switched course a few months later, with CEO, Andy Jassy, writing to employees:

"Instead of specifying that people work a baseline of three days a week in the office, we're going to leave this decision up to individual teams. This decision will be made team by team at the Director level. We expect that there will be teams that continue working mostly remotely, others that will work some combination of remotely and in the office, and still others that will decide customers are best served having the team work mostly in the office. We're intentionally not prescribing how many days or which days—this is for Directors to determine with their senior leaders and teams."[3]

Of course, this policy switch also begs an important question: How will that work? How will directors and their teams make those decisions? Flexible schedules are difficult to figure out, they come with risks, like burnout, and they force decisions on already common problems, like schedules overrun by meetings—so how do you deal with all that? (The process we describe in this chapter is all about figuring out that *how*.)

It's not hard to understand why companies are struggling with this. Flexible work can feel like the Wild West to a lot of people, a lawless, chaotic place that's impossible to manage. This is especially true in cultures that have long discouraged flexible arrangements. A blanket policy declaring certain days to be in-office time is concrete and easy to understand (even if the purpose behind it makes less sense). But it really doesn't have to be the Wild West if you create the right kind of framework for your flexible work strategy. The best way forward is to strike a balance between top-down guidance about what's important to your company and empowering teams to figure out what works best for them within that framework. Striking that balance requires trust, transparency, and some new tools.

In Step 3 we cover one such tool that will help you bridge the disconnect between executives and employees, and create a path from principles and guardrails to tangible changes in behaviors and actions: the Team-Level Agreement. What it is, why you need it, and how to go about creating and implementing agreements across a large organization is what this step is about.

"People are looking for both flexibility and trust—to believe that their leaders and the company trust that they can get the work done."

— *Kelly Ann Doherty, Chief People Officer, Mr. Cooper*[4]

What Are Team-Level Agreements?

We've talked about your flexible work purpose and principles, and we've given you insight into how you can put guardrails in place to ensure that you create a level playing field with your flexible work strategy. So far we have mostly focused on high-level decisions made by executives (but with input from people at all levels of the organization).

Now it's time to take your principles and guardrails and put them into practice. How do teams, and the individuals within those teams, translate your organization-wide principles and guardrails into everyday actions? What does it actually look like to work flexibly on a daily basis?

It's a challenging question. After all, it's important to know that you need to keep the playing field level for everyone, but how do you do that when everyone is working in different places and on different schedules? Maintaining a strong sense of community and belonging is important to your organization, but how do you do that for someone who is new to the company and hasn't met anyone yet? Or if all your team members are working on different schedules?

We have a tool to help you sort all this out called the Team-Level Agreement (TLA). Sometimes called "Team working agreements" or "Team operating manuals," TLAs are a set of guidelines or "norms" that establish expectations for how all members of a team will work together. Remember, the vast majority of workers want flexibility, especially schedule flexibility, but they also want guidance. When surveyed by Future Forum, nearly two-thirds of knowledge workers (65.6%) said they want a balance between full flexibility and a predictable framework compared to a rigid schedule or one that had no structure whatsoever (which is why our approach is to create "flexibility within a framework"). Team-level agreements are a way of continuing to build that framework with the goal of inspiring trust, creating clarity, and unlocking performance by being more explicit about how *each team* chooses to operate.

That brings us to a question that comes up often about this: Why *team-level* agreements? Why not an organization-wide agreement? Why not create a single set of guidelines in the same way that we created a single set of principles in Step 1?

Because all teams have different goals and constraints, what works for one team may not work for another. For example:

- Some teams, like Product Development, may need intense periods of in-sync work—say, a few days at the start of each month—followed by more individual, focused time the rest of the month with just a few hours of overlap each day.

- Some teams, like sales or customer support, may need more continuous availability to address issues during the day.

- Some teams are more cross-functional in nature so they have to balance the norms and schedules of multiple teams—think strategy teams or project management.

Of course, organizations will need to define for themselves what "team" means within their organizations. For some, a TLA may work on a broader level, like among individual departments or groups, if the employees within those broader units have similar needs and functions. The main idea here is to give people autonomy, within a framework, to define clearly what works best for them and what will help unlock their potential, both as individuals and as a group.

Where to Start

Each team will need to create their own TLA that meets the unique needs of their members and function. But, because this will be a new task for most people, top-level leaders will need to provide a starting place: a template agreement with guidance about what's important to the organization but flexible enough to allow each team to personalize it.

This doesn't mean that leaders create a set of concrete rules—like Mondays, Tuesdays, and Thursdays are in-office days. It means they begin by working through what guidance is appropriate for their organization in order to create a framework for teams to work within. This document is where you begin to strike that balance between the company's objectives and the needs of the people inside it—and get very explicit about what that looks like for teams on a day-to-day basis.

What Team-Level Agreements Are, and What They Are **Not**

What Team-Level Agreements are:

- A guided look at how to turn your company's flexible principles into everyday norms and behaviors.

- What guidance looks like: lots of examples that are specific to the organization—give options to choose from!

Example: At RBC, guidance around their principle that "proximity still matters" might appear in their TLA template this way:

"Teams should think about the frequency in which they will commit to getting together in-person in order to best support their work.

e.g. One week each quarter for roadmap planning.

e.g. A day or two each week to connect and build deeper relationships (perhaps especially for newer teams)."

Example: At Genentech (a company you'll learn more about in the next chapter), guidance around schedule flexibility might appear this way:

"Team members should work with their managers to determine what schedule best balances their individual needs with those of the team. As they do this, they should focus not just on where they will work, but also on the when and the how.

e.g. Available options for when people work can include: a regular work week, a compressed work week, and flexible start-stop times (i.e. two hours in the mornings before the kids go to school, at least two hours to overlap with their teams mid-day, and other time as needed to get their jobs done).

e.g. Available options for how people work can include: full time, part time, job sharing, and flex retirement."

What Team-Level Agreements are *not*:

Top-down mandates:

Example: "Mondays, Tuesdays, and Thursdays are in-office days for everyone."

Or worse,

"Executives must commit to one day a week in the office; junior employees must be in the office five days a week."

If creating a TLA sounds tricky, don't worry: we'll get you started and walk you through the process. In the toolkit at the back of this book (page 185), you will find that starting place, basically a template for your template, or what we call our *starter template*. It was built based on Slack's own Digital-First efforts, and you will use it to create a working template that's specific to your organization—one that you can send out to your teams along with guidance about how they can make flexibility work for them.

We'll start by walking you through the basics of what might be in your TLA, covering some of the most common categories of agreement that we've seen across a wide-range of organizations. We will also provide specific examples of norms that you can choose from or use to inspire your own. As you read, remember that our starter template is designed to be adapted. You will be modifying it, adding sections or deleting categories, to meet your organization's needs. Then your leaders and their teams will be doing the same with the template that you provide them and continuing to evolve it over time. After all, business is not static, so neither should any document that defines how it works.

Our starter template has five categories to kick things off:

1. Values
2. Schedules and Meetings
3. Accountability
4. Relationships
5. Checking In

We will take you through these categories one by one. Then, at the end of this step, we will cover some best practices for rolling this tool out and creating agreements throughout your organization.

A Reminder Before You Get Started

In order to keep a level playing field, your team norms should accommodate a wide range of situations, including team members who are:

- Both new to the company and have been with you for years.
- Fresh out of school and seasoned professionals (and everyone in between).

- Introverted, extroverted, or both depending on the situation.
- From a diverse range of backgrounds in terms of race, gender, religion, and personal experience.
- Coming from a wide range of home situations, from single and living alone to multigenerational households filled with all ages (and everything in between).
- At all levels and in all functions of the organization.

The aim is to leave no talent behind!

Values: What Do We Value in Our Working Environment as a Team?

We once had a client who knew they wanted to create a flexible work plan, but they were struggling to figure out what flexible work would actually *look* like on a daily basis in their company. They were stuck at this very stage, and we agreed to come in and give them a TLA workshop.

We worked with a group of executives who were trying to figure out how to create a template agreement to send to teams throughout their organization. They understood that their people wanted flexibility, but because they were so used to having set schedules with clear parameters, that's where they began their discussions.

- "Should our requirement be that people come into the office a minimum of two days a week or three?"
- "*Requirement* doesn't sound like a very flexible word. Should we call it a *guideline*?"
- "*Guideline* isn't strong enough. How about *expectation*?"
- "Or maybe *strongly recommended*."

It was the wrong starting place. No matter what they called it, they were starting with a rule that would *limit* flexibility (particularly the kind of schedule flexibility that more people want) not support it. This is why, once again, we are asking you to think about what you're aiming for before you start determining guidelines or norms that may or may not support that aim. If your flexible work purpose is to unlock potential in your people, then start with what's important to those people. What do *they* value?

To spur discussion on this topic, you may find that your company's flexible work principles are a useful guide. Consider them and then ask how team members would finish the following statement:

As a team, we value working in an environment that . . . [fill in the blank].

Some common examples include:

- Allows everyone to participate fully whether in-person or remote
- Encourages continuous feedback
- Prioritizes and honors focus time

Spell out the answers clearly and concisely in your TLA. Clear and concise are key here and throughout the agreement. Remember our advice in Step 1 when we asked you to define your Flexible Work Principles? We asked you to *keep it simple*. That means a handful of values are better than several dozen. Things like principles and values can feel like heady, illusive concepts, so the more complicated you make them, the harder it will be for people to appreciate them.

Schedules and Meetings: How Will We Collaborate?

This category may be the longest and most involved for many teams because of ingrained habits and behaviors around our calendars, so we break it up into two parts: schedules and meetings. We know from research that schedule flexibility is what's most important to people, and yet these are two areas where it is often limited in traditional workplaces. Schedule flexibility is new territory for a lot of people, so it might take some time and experimentation to find what works best for your teams. It will likely take some time, too, to get into new habits. As one group we worked with said when trying to adopt new norms around meetings: "Everyone here feels like they have to be in the meeting if they're invited, or they want to be in the meeting if they're not. We all have FOMO (fear of missing out)!" Old habits can be hard to break, but being explicit about the behaviors you want, and writing them down in this agreement so you can hold each other accountable, will help.

Schedules

A flexible schedule is not the same as having no schedule at all. Team members still need time together when they can collaborate, debate, or exchange information. But that doesn't mean they need to be available for these things for the entire workday.

Rather than having set "working hours," what we've found works best in most cases is for teams to set what's called "core collaboration hours." This is generally an agreed-upon three-to-four hour timespan during the day when team members can expect to be "live" and available to one another for things like meetings or requests for feedback.

By focusing on shorter bursts of collaboration time (versus the standard office norm of "working hours from 9-to-5"), you unlock a lot more productivity as a team. In fact, human communication is typically "bursty"—meaning that it naturally alternates between periods of high activity and periods of little to no activity at all—according to Anita Woolley and Chiristoph Riedl writing in the *Harvard Business Review:* "Our research suggests that such bursts of rapid-fire communications, with longer periods of silence in between, are hallmarks of successful teams."[5]

This approach allows more flexibility for individuals who may prefer starting their day early, or those who might have caregiving responsibilities in the afternoon and prefer more focus time in the evening. You also prevent people from feeling like they have to be "on" and responsive all the time (which can result in burnout), and ensure that they have periods each day for focused work. As Chief People Officer, Melanie Collins, put it when Dropbox instituted core collaboration hours as part of their flexible work strategy: "The intent of this setup is to encourage non-linear workdays where employees gain more control of their time and have more time for things like deep work."

When deciding the optimal window for collaboration hours, consider things like:

- Team members' various time zones. First thing in the morning East Coast time isn't going to work well if you have team members on the West Coast or even in different time zones around the globe.

- Individual preferences for morning or afternoon meetings. Are some team members parents whose children will be home from school in the late afternoons, making collaboration more difficult? Are some simply not morning people, making a midday collaboration more effective?

- The amount of individual, focused work vs. collaborative work that team members tend to engage in. Teams that do a lot of solo work may need fewer collaboration hours and may even want to set aside one or more meeting-free days during the week.

- In some cases, core collaboration hours may vary early in the week versus later in the week, depending on the needs and wishes of the team.

An example of how norms around core collaboration hours could show up in your TLA would be:

As a team, we have the following norms around our schedules . . .

- **Core collaboration hours:** We expect team members to be available for in-sync work between the hours of 10:00 a.m.–2:00 p.m. PT, Mondays through Thursdays (a core collaboration hour example from a US-based team balancing West Coast and East Coast members).

Or, for global teams:

- **Core collaboration hours:** We expect team members to be available during four-hour windows each day for synchronous collaboration, aligned to timezone (refer to the illustration on page 13, which Dropbox used to explain this norm to employees).

Some more key areas to consider when deciding on schedule norms are:

- Do we need or want to craft a separate norm around dedicated focus time (not just collaboration hours)? Sometimes one is enough, and sometimes teams appreciate being as explicit as possible so that there is no misunderstanding across people. Example: We prioritize and dedicate two-hour focus time blocks from 1:00 p.m.–3:00 p.m., every weekday.

- Can we be more proactive about focus time distractions, like notifications, and set new expectations across the team? Example: We default to notifications off during non-core collaboration hours or focus time.

- Can we minimize individuals feeling like they need to be "on all the time" by being intentional about our expectations regarding response times? Example: We set clear expectations for who needs to respond and when, and we reserve off-hours escalations for truly urgent issues, via text or phone call.

Meetings

As we discussed in the last step, better meeting hygiene is a universal need to make all work, and not just flexible work, more successful. Being in back-to-back meetings (whether digitally or in-person) is the complete opposite of schedule flexibility, but is often the reality of so many of our work days. The aim here is to enable norms above—like "core collaboration hours" within a four-hour timespan—by being more effective and efficient in how you spend your time together as a team (remember that 70% of senior managers believe meetings are unproductive and inefficient)[6] while also being conscious of keeping a level playing field so that your norms don't disadvantage certain groups.

Start by rethinking your meeting culture: What are common habits that your team engages in when meeting? How are they working? How do people feel about them? We talked before about how Dropbox uses what they call their "Three D" model for planning meetings: debate, discuss, decide (and our addition: development). If you're not doing at least one of those four things, then you're probably better off communicating in some other way that doesn't require blocking off time on everyone's calendar. That could appear in a TLA in the following way:

- Meetings should be for when team members need to engage in the Four Ds—discuss, debate, decide, develop. If you're not doing that, then we should cancel the meeting.

Depending on your team members, it might also be important to consider how (or if) you use video for meetings. Research has shown that videoconferencing can leave people feeling fatigued—more so than if they had just attended an in-person meeting or conference call.[7] Reducing the use of video can not only mitigate this problem, but it also helps level the playing field for individuals who might not have the ideal video-on situation at home, like moms with young kids or younger people and city-dwellers who are less likely to have room at home for a dedicated office space. Guidance that supports that could be:

- No video will be used for one-on-one conversations or afternoon meetings.

These kinds of norms will be new to many people. They will disrupt the traditional ways in which they've been working since the beginning of their careers. We've found that productive meeting and communications hygiene requires regular practice and pruning. "Meeting-creep" happens all too easily, and teams find it useful to dedicate regular time (e.g. monthly or quarterly) to reviewing how they're doing and where they can be more proactive in decreasing meeting load and related video-conference fatigue while increasing dedicated focus time for deep work.

Some more examples of norms that companies could adopt around meetings are:

As a team, we have the following norms around our meetings and communication expectations . . .

- We commit to creating agendas at least 24 hours in advance for all live meetings.
- Notes from meetings are always documented and shared back to the team.
- More than two of us invited to another internal team's meeting? Others should feel free to decline.
- Ensure that there's a clear owner or decision maker for work. Then you don't need 10 people from the same team in the meeting.
- Ensure that there's a regular habit of sharing notes and documenting decisions that come out of discussions, so there's less meeting FOMO and people can find out what happened in their own time.

Accountability: How Do We Hold Each Other Accountable?

For flexible work to be successful, teams need to measure success by outcomes, not by how many hours someone works in a day, or by how many meetings someone attends (which further supports the guidelines around meetings that we just talked about). To do that, teams need to focus on defining outcomes, roles, and responsibilities upfront and communicating as changes and different needs arise.

This is such an important topic that we devote an entire chapter to it (see Step 6). For now, understand that this topic will likely show up in your TLAs. See the following examples to start thinking about how to drive accountability in a flexible work environment:

As a team, we want to set expectations and hold each other accountable in the following ways . . .

- We clearly define work and deliverable requirements from the beginning, including a primary owner (also known as a "directly responsible individual" or DRI).

- We commit to making it clear when we need feedback from whom and by when.

- Every major project will have retrospective meetings to reflect on what went well, what could've been better, and what we've learned.

Relationships: Coming Together as a Team

One of the most common concerns about flexible work that we hear from executives is that it will negatively impact company culture. Many organizations have spent a whole lot of resources on creating programs and redesigning their offices in an effort to foster a sense of camaraderie and belonging among their people. Their leaders end up wondering: "What will happen to our culture if we aren't in the office?"

This is an important topic, which is why (once again) we cover it in detail in its own chapter (Step 5). While executives need to be thinking about how to build connection across a flexible organization, which is what we'll focus on in that chapter, individual teams can play a part too by being explicit about what will help build relationships among their fellow team members. Some examples to start thinking about:

As a team, we want to build our relationships with each other in the following ways . . .

- When it comes to bringing ourselves to work, we embrace vulnerability with boundaries. We operate from a place of trust. We can speak openly about our lives outside of work.

- We commit to celebrating one another's successes both publicly and within the team.

- We commit to being open and honest about when we are overloaded or need support, both personally and professionally.

Note: In the beginning of this process, when team members are getting accustomed to new norms, it's best to focus first on building connection within your immediate team. Over time, however, consider expanding these agreements to finding ways to intentionally connect with other teams across the organization—by bringing in more regular guest speakers to team meetings, for example, or supporting more cross-team mentorship with senior leaders.

Checking-in: Evolving Our Team Agreements Over Time

Finally, teams will need freedom to experiment with operating norms that help them stay aligned as a group while still maintaining flexibility for individuals. No first draft of this agreement should be set in stone, but rather reconsidered regularly to ensure that the norms team members agreed on actually support their work, instead of getting in the way of it. Because we have asked you to start off simply, with just a few norms to get used to at a time, teams may find they need to add more as they go and discover what works. Or, they may end up simplifying, finding that too many norms are counterproductive. And even when no changes are necessary, regular check-ins will help ensure your team stays aligned on this front, especially as objectives change and team members come and go. The TLA is meant to be a flexible document that can grow and change with your business. Some examples are:

As a team, we want to check in on how things are going by . . .

- Spending part of our team meeting every month discussing our team-level agreements and getting feedback on what is and isn't working.
- Creating a quarterly poll to get anonymous feedback across our department on our TLAs, and suggestions for improvement.

The Process: How to Use Our Starter Template to Get Agreement

It often doesn't work very well to simply send out our starter template TLA to a large number of teams and let them figure things out from there.

For one reason, a lot of people will have never seen something like this before, so providing context for it is important.

For another, you will want to think through your priorities and parameters before letting teams create their own agreements. If you simply send out a starter TLA without first thinking through what's important to your organization, you may have teams going in directions you don't support. For example, suppose a team decides they will be completely remote, with only a few hours of collaboration time each week. Those decisions may run counter to your desire to continue building a strong culture and an environment that prioritizes collaboration—which requires a larger investment in time together, in a digital space at the least, if not also occasionally in person. But once a team has decided on their norms, it's difficult to backtrack and reverse their decisions without making them feel like their efforts and opinions didn't matter. That's not the tone you want to strike right off the bat when creating this kind of change within your organization.

Instead, take our starter template and use it to create a flexible TLA that's specific to your company and makes clear its objectives, while still providing teams with relevant examples and options, as a framework in which they can make decisions. You aren't making all the decisions for them; you're aiming simply to get them thinking in a new way, show them what's possible, and provide guidance about what may be going too far.

Follow these best practices to create your organization's own template TLA and then cascade it from there:

1. Customize our starter template for your organization
2. Create early champions for change by piloting with a few teams
3. Disseminate to additional teams with context and guidance
4. Create a way for teams to give feedback and share best practices

Customize Our Starter Template for Your Organization

Are there teams within your organization that are already working flexibly and doing it well? For most companies there are, and that's a good place to start. Find out what has worked for them and what hasn't and pull from them examples that are relevant to your organization. Revisit your principles and remind yourself what's important to you. Is there specific guidance that you want to set? For example: core collaboration hours need to be at least three-hour chunks of time. Or: teams should plan virtual or in-person gatherings at least once a month to foster a sense of camaraderie and belonging.

Create Early Champions for Change by Piloting with a Few Teams

You probably have some idea about which high-performing and innovative teams within your organization would be good test subjects for this. In some companies we've worked with, executives have started with their own teams to pilot the project and provide feedback, which is a great way to lead by example. Either way, the idea is to battle test the template. What categories are most important, missing, or unnecessary? What questions come up when a team tries to fill it out? Make adjustments to your company's template based on what you learn and seed it with examples that are specific to your company.

Disseminate to Additional Teams with Context and Guidance

When you send out TLA templates to your teams, provide them with context and try to anticipate some of their questions. The most common ones are: *What is this? Why are we doing it? How will it help our team specifically? Is it required? Where do we go if we have questions or need help? What do we do when we've finished it?* In general, you want to create a communications plan around your TLAs that sets people up for success. Be intentional about the narrative you use to set the context about what these team agreements are for. For example, one company we worked with called it "an opportunity to rethink meeting culture that didn't work"—a concept just about everyone in the organization could get behind. (Note: Team leaders will need their own guidance for figuring out how to create these agreements with their teams. See the next section for more on this.)

Create a Way for Teams to Give Feedback and Share Best Practices

TLAs are meant to evolve with the needs of your people and your business. To enable this, you have to create a way for teams to provide you with feedback so you can update your template or guidance as needed. It should also be a way for teams to share with each other. As one of our clients said, "make it viral" by creating a space where teams can show what's working for them and what isn't, share their learnings, and discuss different outcomes. Then other teams can use that information to more organically adapt the template to their own needs. Some companies, in fact, like Slack and Genentech, make all their TLAs public so anyone in the company can see them and compare, which is a great way to support the practice and build the kind of culture you want. As Rachael Allison, People Strategy Lead at Genentech, says: "Our people strategy is radical transparency, so not only do we want the agreements, but we want everyone in the company to be able to find them and know what they are. After all, if you want to go shopping for a job within the company, you should be able to see what the agreements are first, so you have a better idea of what it's like to work with that group of people."

Guidance for Your Team Leaders

There isn't one right way to approach TLAs as a team leader, but we do suggest when you disseminate your organization's TLA template, that you provide them with some guidance.

First, make it clear that this is a document that should be **co-created** with their team members. The intention is not for team leaders to set "the rules" and then hand out the TLA as if it's a rulebook for team members to follow. In order to gain alignment within the team and to ensure that the agreement has the intended effect of enabling individuals to do their best work within a flexible framework, the entire team needs to take part in creating it.

There are different ways to approach this, and team leaders will have to find what works for them. The following are some suggested steps to take that have worked for others:

First, introduce the template to the team, especially the large categories, and set the context for why you're doing this. For example: "Flexible work means that we aren't all in the office at the same time anymore, so it's more important than ever that we be explicit about HOW we work together."

Second, let team members choose which category they want to "own," making sure all team members participate, and then allow them some time on their own to write down their ideas. They can think about both current norms and aspirational ones by answering these two questions:

- What do we currently do here that we like?
- What do we want to be doing that could help us work more effectively together?

Third, bring the team back together to discuss what each sub-team came up with. (Note: Per our advice about good meeting hygiene, it's best to share each sub-team's ideas beforehand, so people can read in advance.) Discuss, push, challenge. Use this as an opportunity to refine your agreement while keeping the following advice in mind.

- It's never a good idea to create a ten-page list of norms. It's too much change all at once and will make it harder for people to make the necessary adjustments.
- Instead, prioritize what's most important and start there. Begin with a limit of 2–3 norms under each category.

Fourth, be explicit and write down what you agree to in order to create clarity. A manager we know once told us that he kept telling his team members they didn't need to ask her permission if they wanted to leave early for an appointment or take an hour off in the middle of the day; they could just do it! But she was surprised to find that they kept asking his permission anyway. This continued until the team finally sat down together and wrote out their flexible-schedule norms. "No one asked for permission again after that," she said. "There's something about putting it down on paper that creates a shared expectation across the whole team and unlocks that freedom and flexibility for people."

- Don't assume a conversation is enough. Write down what you agree to.
- Be clear and concise. Make sure everyone understands what's been agreed to before you move on. And, as a leader, don't be afraid to repeat yourself to make sure the message gets through.

Fifth, build these norms into your team's processes by doing things like:

- Determine how you'll hold each other accountable for these norms. For example, you might consider blocking your calendars during non-collaboration hours.

- Determine how frequently and by what method you'll revisit these norms to update or adjust them. You might also decide how team members can escalate when something isn't working for them.

- Share these norms with teams that work closely with yours. Not only will this start to cascade learnings across different teams (something we'll talk more about in Step 4), but it also helps other teams collaborate better with yours by finding the best ways to bridge the expectations your team has set with their own—around things like how and when to set meetings with you, how they escalate issues on cross-functional work, and so on.

- Make them part of your onboarding process for every new employee. At Genentech, Allison says, "We tell everybody in our Welcome to Genentech package to go ask for their team's agreement, to review it, and to make sure they understand it with their peers and their manager."

- And then just go! Try it out. See what works and what doesn't. Make changes as necessary. And remember to support your people along the way, as they adjust to this new way of working.

That final point leads us to the next step. Because this is a new way of working for most people, one that requires new principles, guardrails, and norms to support it, you will need to put in place structures and processes that allow people to ask questions, share best practices, and generally experiment, learn, and adjust as they discover what works best for themselves, their team, and their organization as a whole. That's what we'll talk about in Step 4: Experiment and Learn.

Checklist for Step 3: Commit to How You'll Work

☑ Have you reviewed our starter TLA template to understand what might be included and what it takes to create one?

☑ Have you engaged in discussions and gotten everyone on your own team involved in creating a TLA that works for your group?

☑ Have you started to cascade this practice throughout your organization by providing a company-specific template populated with your own examples and providing team leaders with guidance for creating ones with their teams?

☑ Have you put a plan in place for regularly reviewing and updating TLAs within your own team and throughout the organization to ensure they always support the work?

Step 4: Experiment, Experiment, Experiment: Normalize a Culture of Learning

It should be clear by now that flexible work is a real change for most people and most companies, and the changes required go well beyond simply allowing employees to WFH a day or two each week. After the pandemic hit, we spent a lot of time talking with executives about why so many were focused on getting people back into the office as soon as possible—especially considering all the evidence showing that most companies had been quite successful without it.

Much of what we heard came down to two things: fear and habit. "There's a lot of fear of the unknown; fear that the culture they came up in will 'degrade,'" explained one executive, whose sentiments echoed much of what we heard elsewhere. "There's also an underlying presumption that the past was good, when it wasn't uniformly." It may have been good for most executives, but, as we've seen, the way work was done in the past wasn't for everybody. The question becomes how do you make a shift this significant happen, especially when some people—especially those in decision-making positions—are personally happy with how things were before?

It will require a process of experimenting, learning, and making adjustments in both behavior and thinking if you want it to stick, and not everything is going to work perfectly from the start. This has been true at Genentech, a biotech company that has led the way on workplace flexibility since 2018, when they first built a formal flexible work program. Those early efforts had the backing of top-level leaders because of the opportunity to make more efficient use of their real estate. But, perhaps for that reason, they became largely focused on location flexibility, not schedule flexibility, which limited the appeal, especially to parents who struggled with the demands of fixed schedules. As Rachael Allison, Genentech's People Strategy Lead, explains, "Working flexibly became synonymous in the company with 'working from home,' so we were losing a lot of the other flexible options that could really help people."

Still, they got a head start on flexible work before it became a critical issue during the pandemic, and that meant that they got a chance to experiment and learn things early compared to many other companies. In a company full of research scientists, it's no surprise that Genentech did a lot of testing of their new workplace concepts, gathering data, and measuring outcomes. They learned that most of their employees wanted flexibility, but that didn't mean they wanted to WFH full time. Instead they wanted the flexibility of choice—within certain parameters, of course, so they could continue to collaborate with colleagues. The data also began to show that teams with structured flexibility were having success and the program found some champions among progressive groups. But despite having all of that data about employee preference and pockets of success, prior to the pandemic, Genentech only reached an estimated 300 people successfully adopting flexible arrangements of some kind, a modest number on their 10,000-person campus, and that's where the program stalled.

The culprit was what one leader described as "the frozen middle." There was a sizable group who didn't see any reason to change—many of whom had roots in academia and had worked their way up through traditional workplace structures, earning their titles and office space with a view along the way. They'd always believed that work was best done in person because that's the way they'd always done it. How could they know that flexible work could actually succeed if they'd never seen it happen in their own teams?

But then the pandemic hit and something interesting happened. Offices shut down and many people were forced to become more flexible. Suddenly the company—and the whole world, in fact—was gathering lots of data about how successful flexible work can be.

Allison remembers that being key to finally beginning to thaw the frozen middle. There was one top executive who had real concerns about making such major changes to the way they worked. Allison and her team were looking for ways to build her confidence, so they went to two of her senior staffers, one of whom was a research scientist who had been with the company for years and had never embraced flexibility. But when presented with evidence gathered during the pandemic, showing the positive effect on both productivity and engagement, he changed his mind. As Allison put it, "He became a believer." What's more, "He became a believer who could sway others with the evidence." With the help of the project team, he did just that. The senior executive he worked under became a convert as well. After that, their group quickly got their TLAs in place and hit the ground running. It was a quick shift once they got started, but, considering that their flexible work program started back in 2018, it was also one that was years in the making.

The moral of this story is that there will be no perfect data point or external benchmark that will convince everyone that flexible work will work. Radical change can be scary, so you need to build evidence that it can work locally. It takes a mix of a little leap of faith to allow experimentation, executive support to prototype new ways of working, and a willingness to learn your way toward habits and practices that work for your people. Genentech had the advantage of experimenting with flexibility pre-pandemic, so when the moment came, they were able to accelerate the pace of change.

By now you have some key elements in place—your principles, your guardrails, your TLAs—but figuring out how to implement something that requires a real shift in people's beliefs and behavior can still feel daunting, especially since there's no single blueprint for making it happen. After all, when Genentech started their journey, they never could have anticipated where they'd be today or what would get them there.

Like them, you have to experiment and learn, stay agile and make adjustments (because not every experiment is going to work on the first try), and communicate every step of the way to bring people along. It won't happen all at once, which is why this chapter is going to help you figure out how to build momentum and support as you move forward and figure out how to make it work.

Build Momentum for Change

In Step 2 we told you about IBM's "Work From Home Pledge" and how it grew out of spontaneous conversations people started to have about the struggle to balance personal and professional responsibilities. It took a global pandemic to ignite the conversation, but it proved useful beyond that. People started asking questions about why we work the way we do. There are a whole set of norms that most of us follow at work, but how often have we stopped to ask why, or if they even make sense? Why are we so attached to meetings? Why do we suspect that someone working from a different location or on a different schedule isn't working just as hard as everyone else? Why do we feel like we have to put on an uncomfortable shirt just because someone is going to see us for half an hour on video? Are these things really useful and productive or are they just habits and assumptions?

Allison talked about one such situation at Genentech that could have benefited from closer examination. One group had a mandatory, in-person staff meeting at 4:00 p.m. on Fridays, which meant two things: anyone attending that meeting would miss the Genentech bus home *and* they would surely get stuck in terrible traffic as they'd have to leave at prime commute time. Why? And, as Allison asked, "Who did it support?" It certainly didn't support parents of school-age kids because it meant some employees weren't getting home until late in the evening.

These are good examples of how top-down mandates often fail. For flexible work to work, leadership has to be involved, they have to lead by example, and they have to ensure that critical investments are made so the work can succeed. But when you take a purely top-down approach you get the kind of overly rigid and yet non-specific (in terms of purpose, anyway) mandates like "Everyone must come to the office on Mondays, Tuesdays, and Thursdays" or "Everyone must be here at 4:00 p.m. on Fridays for staff meetings." Instead, you need to make room for people to experiment with what works, create systems for sharing successes and failures, and build momentum through best practices and champions. The IBM Pledge, for example, was completely employee-driven. CEO, Arvind Krishna, simply had the foresight to embrace the work those employees had already done and share it broadly, as an example of best practices for their organization, but also as a signal about the kind of place IBM is and the kind of people they want working there.

Remember this as you move forward: Organizational change requires an organization full of people to make it happen. This will mean thinking differently and getting your people to do the same, by finding ways to get them involved and communicating so all your people get the message.

Find Early Champions and Change Advocates

In previous steps we talked about the importance of involving people from all areas and levels of your organization in designing your flexible work plans—even in Step 1, when defining your principles. This is an ongoing need that requires putting structures in place to ensure it happens. A good way to start is by forming a permanent task force by enlisting representatives who can offer different perspectives, test new ways of working, share best practices, and help shape the path forward.

At Slack, our Digital-First task force was formed by having each of our CEO's direct reports nominate a leader from their department. The commitment was made clear: each member was asked to dedicate at least 20% of their time to the work, including weekly meetings. Others in key functions were asked to participate—like internal and external communications (so internal and external narratives would be consistent), HR (to weigh in on employment, legal, learning, and development issues), Workplace (to help reimagine how our facilities would be used), IT (to facilitate new tools and technologies that might be needed), and Program Management (to help with operations)—with an eye toward creating change that would cascade through the entire company. And finally, it's critical that the group has a senior representative who could connect the task force's work and questions directly to executive leadership. Brian was the senior executive who led the group and reported back to the CEO and executive team, ensuring that the task force's work was not done in a vacuum and mitigating any potential disconnects between the two groups along the way.

Because the goal is to make work better for *everyone* (and not just executives—remember the "great disconnect" we talked about in Step 2), beyond the core task force team, representatives were drafted across different functions, geographies, and demographics, with particular attention paid to gender, racial, and ethnic representation, as well as leaders from employee resources groups like LGBTQIA, Abilities, and Veterans, to help ensure the creation of a truly level playing field. They acted as sounding boards, weighing in on policy drafts, concerns, and ideas, not just to provide feedback, but also—crucially—to help us anticipate how efforts might fail.

The task force's stated mission:

> Make Slack a world-class example for the Digital-First future of work. Blend our narrative, practices and product so that our employees, customers, and partners can all envision a Digital-First future with Slack at its center.

We recommend that all organizations form a diverse task force to drive this change. The following guidance will help:

- Your task force should be composed of respected leaders and change agents, as well as people willing to ask hard questions.

- Both company leaders and task force members need to recognize this work as a real investment. It requires a sizable dedication of time and resources, and isn't just something you attend to occasionally in between other responsibilities.

- Task force members should identify and draw from teams that are already trying new ways of working or willing to experiment. For example, the task force at Slack engaged our Future Forum team; groups within Product, Design and Engineering; and Customer Experience Specialists for pilot projects, experimentation, and feedback.

- Those who are working to create this change need to be supported by dedicated resources from core groups—like internal communications (to help spread the word) and learning and development specialists (to help figure out and teach others what works)—who can help scale the effort. They also need executive support on issues around people, policy, tools that require top-level decisions, and resource allocation.

Prototype the Path

Because there's no single blueprint for the future, and because every company is different, what works in one environment may not work in another. This makes it essential that you create a culture that encourages experimentation and sharing—so you can evolve into a flexible workplace that works for everyone and keeps evolving as your business grows and changes.

Of course, it's not easy to create a cultural shift. You have to do more than just tell people you want them to experiment, share, and learn as they go. Complex problems like creating flexibility for people, teams, and organizations requires understanding the needs of the people involved, engaging them in generating ideas, and taking a hands-on approach to prototyping and testing those ideas—a process commonly referred to as Design Thinking.[1] As we learned with Genentech earlier in this chapter, principles and guardrails can only go so far in convincing people to change the way they work. Many times, jumping in and just committing to testing new ideas is the best way to show that flexible work is possible and that it can work even better when you land on a solution that sticks!

Following are the five phases of the Design Thinking Process, which can be applied to creating flexibility.

- **Empathize:** Develop an empathetic understanding of the problem you are trying to solve—what are some of the challenges that people and teams are facing with creating flexibility? You can do this through employee sentiment surveys, focus groups, and diary studies of people at work, or simply through listening sessions with diverse cross-sections of your organization.

- **Define:** Use that research to create a problem statement from your people's perspective (e.g. "We're having a hard time balancing equal voices and participation in a discussion when a majority of people are in a room in the office, and a few are on video conference"), with particular focus on identifying the highest impact challenges. You'll want to test the definitions of the problem with the people you're trying to help.

- **Ideate:** Generate potential solutions. Start with "how might we solve . . ."-type questions. We'd suggest brainwriting (which we discussed in Step 2) over brainstorming for this. And leverage more than just your task force. For example, tap internal best practices: What are your high-performance teams doing?

- **Prototype:** Find low-cost, quick ways to build some of the solutions proposed. Enlist "pilot teams" of those willing to test new methodologies, tools, and processes. Make sure they're supported by IT, facilities, and HR. Oftentimes, task force members and their teams are the best places to start prototyping.

- **Test:** Execute on changes in small scale ways to not only measure results, but further refine your approach. Run iterative tests in pilot teams, or side-by-side comparisons across teams. If you have a global organization, test changes in different countries. Make sure teams know where to share ideas and results, and make it a public forum so that others can learn and contribute.

The five phases aren't necessarily linear. They loop back to each other, building a continuous learning loop (see Figure 4.1).

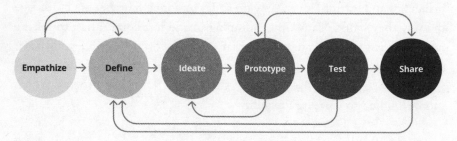

Figure 4.1

Let's use Slack's guardrail of "one dials in, all dial in" as an example of how this can work. That guardrail was developed based on the Empathize phase: Many people, especially historically discriminated groups, were concerned that their need for flexibility would result in an unlevel playing field because presenteeism would give others an unfair advantage. Just about everyone appreciated the purpose behind it, but in a practical sense, how does that actually work?

We took the problem into the **define** phase by talking to people across the organization to better understand the challenges of making these kinds of "hybrid" meetings work. We found that people were having a hard time balancing equal voices and participation in a discussion when a majority of people were in a meeting room, and a few were on video conference.

The task force then started to Ideate on different ways to solve this, but also quickly realized that there were easy ways to **prototype** and **test,** almost as fast as they could **ideate,** by using equipment they already had at hand.

We enlisted a few teams to experiment with different options—literally different setups while video conferencing—with the goal of ensuring that every participant could be seen and heard equally. One of the first things those teams discovered was that if there was a small group together in a conference room while most others dialed in from home, it actually disadvantaged the in-office group. When they used the standard conference room equipment, they didn't have the same access to chat and each person wasn't highlighted on video when they spoke. So experimenters tried a group of people in a conference room, each on their own laptop, while others dialed in. That worked for people dialing in, and having everyone on their own video was great, but inside the conference room there was a terrible echo from multiple mics. Next they tried using just one central laptop for audio while everyone else was muted but could still be seen on screen. That was an improvement, and when using an in-room audio hookup, it worked even better. The group eventually concluded that having video for each individual was key (giving everyone equal ability to be seen, identified by nameplate, access to chat), but with shared audio among those in the same room.

Along the way, the experimenters shared their progress in a public Slack channel, which prompted even more improvements: One employee posted about bringing the laptop stand from her desk to a conference room meeting in order to ease her neck strain. That turned into a way, not just to create a better in-room meeting setup, but also to encourage others to adopt new practices: Laptop stands were placed at each seat in a conference room. Anyone who used the meeting room going forward would be visually reminded to set up their laptop and dial-in directly.

The **ideate** / **prototype** / **test** loops had slowed down at that point— teams that were testing had found a common, workable solution. Because the teams had been doing much of their work in public, in a Slack channel called #discuss-digital-first, it was easier to **share** the findings and best practices more broadly through announcement channels. And the physical reminder of the laptop stands sitting on conference room tables made it easier to drive adoption of the new "one dials in, all dials in" guideline.

This is just one example of how you can apply Design Thinking principles to your future of work efforts. You'll find a framework and example in the Toolkit at the back of the book, so you can apply this method to the challenges that arise as you build a more flexible workplace.

Encourage Experimentation

The findings of the "one dials in, all dial in" experiments were also publicized this way on social media, to both encourage buy-in and get others to share additional ideas that might work even better across other companies and teams who were experimenting:

"So, a group of folks have been experimenting. Here's something that might work, and costs almost nothing. With 2–5 people in a conference room, and others dialed in, try this:

- Everyone's laptop is open, and on a laptop stand; avoids neck strain from looking down at your laptop screen and you've got access to chat, polls, etc.
- One person has open mic and speaker, others are off.
- More than 4–5 people? Use the in-room equipment, but only the mic.

Putting a couple $25 laptop stands in each conference room makes it really easy to remind people about this as well.

Figuring out how to blend together flexible models is going to take experimentation. Start simple, use what you've got, experiment, share feedback (preferably in a public channel) and give people easy ways to do what works—like putting the stands in the room.

What have you tried that works?"

Bring Managers Along for the Ride

Whether it's small experiments like this one or high-level decisions about the principles behind your flexible work strategy, a good rule of thumb for leaders to always keep in mind is to *do your work in public*. Not every little thing, obviously. That would be information overload and some issues need to be worked out before being communicated so you don't confuse people or lead them astray. But it's important that executives and task force members don't sequester ideas, decisions, and thinking for months on end. Giving a sense of where you're going, the progress you're making along the way, and transparently sharing everything you can generates trust and builds momentum. As the author of *Change Monster*, Jeanie Daniel Duck, wrote in *Harvard Business Review*: "When the task force chooses not to inform the rest of the organization about its work it is saying, 'We're busy figuring out your future—we'll tell you what it is when we're ready.'"[2] That sort of information vacuum is sure to build distrust and make it that much harder to win people over when you finally get around to asking them to commit to new ways of working.

This is important to do for your organization as a whole (which we'll talk about in just a moment), but let's first focus on your managers. They're the key to the success of any change management effort because they're on the frontlines. They're the ones who have to make this work day in, day out, so you need to enlist them in the process and support them throughout.

Your managers won't be uniform in their beliefs. Some may be reluctant, even resistant, and would be more comfortable going back to how things were before. You need to start in the same place we started in Step 1 when gaining alignment among your executive team: You need to start with *why*. People need to understand the benefits of what they're doing in order to buy into the need for change and invest their time and energy into making it happen.

When communicating to managers about the *why*, think about it on two levels: the business reason and the personal one. Return to the business purpose that you defined in Step 1 and help managers understand that this is about winning the battle for talent. Flexible work is going to enable them to more easily attract, retain, and engage the best people for their teams. There may be other reasons worth noting as well, depending on your circumstances, like how flexible work can make teams more agile or make it easier to collaborate in an international organization where colleagues are located across the globe. Take the time to make the case and to ensure your managers understand it. (Take note of how Slack talked about their *why* in the next section below.)

At the same time, talk about the personal *why*. Remember that this is about people, after all. It's about making things better for people, so those people can (and want) to do better work. So, talk about how flexible work has made things better for the people in your organization. Share personal stories like some of the ones we've included in this book. We told you how Mike Brevoort no longer had to leave his family behind to get on an airplane 23 times in a year to do his job and what a difference that made to him personally and professionally. Rachael Allison at Genentech talked about how her daughter's schedule changed when she got to high school and she was no longer getting out at the same time each day—instead, she had three different stop times during the week. Who knows why the school decided to do that to parents, but it was a reality Allison had to deal with and schedule flexibility made it possible.

Your managers have surely encountered their own challenges with balancing the often inflexible structure of working life with the typically varying, and sometimes impossible-to-anticipate, demands of life in general. Companies have long tried to fit everyone into a single 9-to-5 box when, as Allison put it, "One size fits nobody." Make those struggles part of the conversation so managers, and everyone else, can picture how a broader range of options can be beneficial both personally and professionally.

Ask Rather Than Tell

One effective approach we've seen leaders use to build buy-in for flexible work across a group of managers is to *ask* rather than *tell*. Two questions to prompt when discussing flexible work with your managers:

1. What do you think are the opportunities with flexible work?
2. What do you think are the challenges?

These questions give managers a chance to reflect on both flexible work positives that they've witnessed directly, *and* a chance to voice their concerns and be heard. Those concerns, by the way, are also important input into the *empathize* step in understanding what are some of the challenges and pain points that you'll need to address with flexible work.

Build the Case

It's not just managers who need to be convinced; it's everyone. This is a big change management effort, and it requires an ongoing commitment of resources and investment from senior leadership to set the tone.

As you build the case for this new way of working across your organization, there are three things to keep in mind:

- Always lead with why
- Don't just talk to people, engage them
- Transparency and humility

Always Lead with Why

Your executives need to understand why. Your managers need to understand why. And every person in your company needs to understand why. As you roll out your new strategy within the company, there has to be conversation, led by top leaders including the CEO, explaining the purpose and benefits of flexible work and sharing your purpose, principles, and guardrails. This conversation needs to continue at the team level with your managers, and it needs to be ongoing. Creating change is an ongoing process, and so is the conversation you need to have about it. Below is an example of the explanation shared with the team at Slack.

Storytelling Our Why: Digital-First Post to All of Slack

Why the Future Is Digital-First

We've received a lot of good questions since sharing our Digital-First principles, and to begin to answer them we want to emphasize *why* we believe in a Digital-First future.

Slack's competitive advantage depends on continuing to build our talented, diverse and globally-distributed team—our digital-first approach is key to this. Research and our own experience back this up in three main ways:

(continued)

- **Digital-First enables companies to access broader, more diverse talent:** There's a giant pool of talent that has been inaccessible by only hiring within a short commute to our offices. Being Digital-First also means employees who work outside "headquarters" can now grow their careers in ways that other companies cannot offer.

- **Flexibility will become a key aspect of hiring and retaining talented people:** Flexibility is now second only to compensation in what matters to employees. We also know that diverse teams outperform their competitors, and flexibility is valued more significantly by some underrepresented groups—notably Black employees and parents/caretakers.

- **Digital-First enables agility and connection:** Going remote didn't slow us down—if anything, we accelerated our performance. Companies that are innovating in processes and tools dramatically outperform laggards in areas like productivity as well as belonging.

Moving to a Digital-First future will come with challenges and require experimentation and patience. But the rewards for our company, customers, and business are fantastic—so let's create it together!

Don't Just Talk to People—Engage Them

You can't rely on only top-down communication to get your point across and drive real change. You have to provide opportunities to engage, like ask-me-anything meetings with executives, publicly open channels (not just for announcements, but for questions and feedback), and team-level conversations. As Duck wrote, "Managing change means managing the conversation between the people leading the change effort and those who are expected to implement the new strategies."[3] In our experience, the most successful route is to provide multiple forums for the conversation to take place: in company-wide meetings, in public channels, and on the team level over the long term.

You can also look for specific areas where you can ask people to get involved. It's often a good idea to start with something that's a common problem across organizations. For example, meetings! We talked already about how meeting-fatigue is a ubiquitous complaint and critical to get right for flexible work to be successful, so open up the discussion and look for solutions together.

Internally we published guidelines for rethinking meetings that started with the most basic question of all: "Do we even need to meet in the first place?" We crowdsourced a lot of the content for meeting guidelines from teams that had already adopted new tools and practices to help alleviate meeting burnout. Our Learning and Development Operational Effectiveness team consolidated and condensed the best ideas into our Meetings Guidelines playbook. This is how those guidelines appeared in our Digital-First Resource guide:

Meeting Hygiene: Do We Need to Meet?

No one grew up dreaming of back-to-back, 9-to-5 meetings, whether virtual or in-person. We know that flexibility when people work makes them more engaged and productive, and that requires developing new muscles around blending synchronous "bursts" together with individual "maker" time. The first step to making space for maker/focus time is to reduce the number of meetings we are collectively in. Always start with—do we really need to meet?

Do We Really Need to Meet?

- **Push status updates to in-channel** and instead use the/remind function or a Workflow to send regular prompts to the team for status updates.

- Similarly, **use a channel to share information** (presentations, documents, etc.) where you're speaking one to many, and instead consider using Stories or a recorded Zoom video to do voiceover for the content.

- Err on the side of **canceling recurring meetings**, or at minimum **ask to cancel if there is no agenda** prior to the meeting.

- Think about **what parts of a meeting can be done asynchronously beforehand** to make the time together more productive (e.g. pre-read, feedback in advance, come up with a set of ideas to bring to the discussion, etc.).

We didn't stop there. We enlisted executives to set the example by canceling recurring meetings that were deemed unnecessary. They also declared a "no meeting week" once a quarter and asked people to use the time to review which meetings they didn't mind missing.

We didn't stop there either. Internal and external feedback about meetings—specifically the burnout people were experiencing around having to book 30 minutes on someone's calendar to have a five-minute conversation—fed our product roadmap. That led to an evolution in our tools and the introduction of "huddles," a voice-only channel in our Slack product. It's for the kind of thing where you might pop into someone's office for a few minutes if you have a quick question or to check-in. You can do the same thing in the Slack product by checking to see if someone is available and then inviting the person to a huddle with just one click. It might take a few minutes to get the information you need, without having to book a time on someone's calendar or risk video-conference fatigue.

Along the way we continually asked for feedback in public channels and opened a specific thread where anyone could offer up ideas:

Have any innovative meeting ideas? We don't have all the answers, and you play an integral role in helping us improve meetings. Share with us in a thread or **#discuss-digital-first** what's working, what's not, and any ideas you have and we'll look to continuously update this resource.

This is just one example of how you can make flexibility work better by communicating openly, getting people involved, and learning and adapting together as an organization.

Transparency and Humility

Embedded in that open call for ideas is a message that's key to our communications strategy: "We don't have all the answers, and you play an integral role in helping us improve." Levi Strauss & Co. took a similar approach. They have long had a regular, all-company, virtual meeting that they call "Chips and Beer" (a play on the name of CEO, Chip Bergh) that's essentially an open forum where employees can talk to leadership about whatever's on their mind. It was at a Chips and Beer meeting that Bergh began talking about the possibility of continuing to work flexibly even after the pandemic. As Chief Human Resources Officer, Tracy Layney, told us, "We basically said, 'We've proven we can work this way, so we're going to figure it out. How it will work, we don't know. The specifics, we don't know. But we're working on it, and more to come'."

People appreciated the fact that they were given insight into what was coming and a chance to weigh in before it happened. Too often leaders resist talking about something that's a work-in-progress and avoid admitting when they don't have all the answers. But that means leaving people in the dark, which is a pretty good way to breed distrust and undermine any change effort.

Leaders also have to be willing to admit when something isn't working as intended and change course. Dell Technologies, which has had a flexible approach to working for over 10 years, decided to do this with a popular policy of "summer hours" that allowed employees to take off at 2:00 p.m. on Fridays during summer months. That is, until Chief Human Resources officer, Jennifer Saavedra, realized that, despite how it sounded, the policy didn't actually support flexibility as well as it could. First of all, it assumed people were working a typical 9-to-5 or 8-to-5 workday, which was antithetical to schedule flexibility. Second, for an international business, it was a very US-centric perspective (in their Australian business units, it was winter during those same months, for example). And finally, it just didn't represent the full spectrum of flexibility. What if someone preferred to take off Tuesday mornings to caretake or exercise, for example? So they got rid of the policy, which was a bit jarring for some. It was a popular program, after all, and at first it felt like something was being taken away. But leaders took it as an opportunity to communicate and engage their people in a deeper conversation about what flexibility really should mean. For some, that meant continuing to log off early on Fridays to enjoy time with family or pursue personal priorities. Others decided that flexibility at other points in the week worked better for them.

Lather, Rinse, Repeat

There is no "done" when creating a better way of working. You're never done experimenting. You're never done learning. And you're never done communicating with people about what you're aiming for and how it's going. This is just good business sense in any change management effort, but it's worth a reminder here because we all tend to lose energy and focus as time passes. This is why it's important to put systems in place for organization-wide and team-level growth and continuing evolution, including the following:

- **Task Force:** A group dedicated to driving flexible work efforts should be permanent and never go away. Rotate in and out members and teams so you can bring in new perspective and energy. Celebrate building your "alumni" base of flexible work leaders. Leverage task force members and pilot participants as champions of the work.

- **Team Level:** Create a schedule for reviewing the norms, habits, and practices within teams, like we talked about in Step 3. As new team members join, new tools and technologies are used, and new objectives are handed down, the needs of the team will change. Just as importantly, habits can get stale, so it's important to review regularly:

  - **Employee Engagement:** Ensure you always have forums open for questions and ideas. Never stop encouraging people to share best practices.

  - **Reward Experimentation:** Don't forget to celebrate your task force members and change advocates who are making a difference. Make sure their work is taken into consideration in compensation and promotions, and that teams who take risks get more visibility and are seen as good teams to work on.

This is how you'll build momentum for change. And that change continues in Step 5, where we'll focus on the new skills and behaviors managers need to adopt to enable flexibility at all levels of your organization.

Checklist for Step 4: Experiment, Experiment, Experiment

☑ Have you formed a task force and identified champions who can drive the change in your organization?

☑ Have you created systems for experimenting with new ways of working as well as for sharing what works and what doesn't?

☑ Have you communicated broadly, openly, and transparently about your flexible work plans and the purpose behind them? Have you reached everyone in your organization and provided them ongoing opportunities to ask questions and provide feedback?

☑ Are you ready to make a continuing investment in finding better ways of working because the change is never "done"?

Step 5: Create a Culture of Connection from Anywhere: Reimagine Your Headquarters

When MURAL's leaders got the news that they had successfully raised $118 million in Series B funding, it was a big moment and cause for celebration. There was only one problem: This was August of 2020, and most of the world was in COVID lockdown.

Most of the company didn't yet know the news, and leaders wanted to stage an event for their people ahead of the public announcement. MURAL is a global company—with offices in Buenos Aires and San Francisco, as well as teams across Europe, Australia, and beyond—but they have always strived for a connected culture. The previous year they'd held a company-wide retreat in Argentina, but traveling was obviously out of the question this time around. So how could they mark this momentous occasion and give their people the party they deserved? Head of Culture and Collaboration, Laïla von Alvensleben, explains, "With only two weeks' notice, I was given the task of creating a unique online event to celebrate our huge achievement, bond with new team members in our fast-growing company and of course, have a fantastic time together."

Pulling that off would require creativity and a lot of intentional planning. MURAL's visual collaboration software can be used for things like virtual brainstorming or "whiteboarding" sessions, so, after von Alvensleben enlisted some help, they naturally started the planning process in a mural. One of the first things they did was decide on a theme: the 2020 MURAL World Tour. Since no one was able to travel in real life, they decided to take their people on a virtual journey around the globe, and beyond.

They continued their planning process with some basic questions about what sort of gathering they wanted to create: What would the experience look and feel like to participants? How could they guide them through the journey in a way that made them feel connected and invested? What did they need to do to make it feel more "real?" This kind of event was largely new territory, so the answers were far from obvious.

"To make participants connect with each other and feel fully immersed in the destinations" was a key goal, so the planning team came up with some novel tactics. They provided Zoom backgrounds for everyone ahead of time by finding relevant images online and bundling them into a folder for download. This was so, during each phase of their "journey," it would look and feel like they were all in the same place. Then they sent out packages to everyone's home with physical props they could use on the day. Items like disco lights and glow sticks were included to foster the sense of celebration.

Physical invitations were sent out ahead of time as well, asking everyone to join together for their world tour. An itinerary was planned—each with its own Zoom background—starting in a virtual "airport lounge" as the gathering site, and then continuing on to a snowy mountain retreat, a tropical island, and finally into outer space. There were unique events planned at each destination, as well as props to go with it—sunscreen and a fan for the tropical island, for example, and astronaut snacks for the trip into space.

On the day of the event, the planning team acted as hosts, even dressing the part as pilots and flight attendants. Once everyone got to the Zoom departure gate, CEO and cofounder, Mariano Suarez-Battan, made the announcement about their newly secured funding (cue glow sticks and disco lights!). The effect worked. Participants said it really felt like they were celebrating together in the same place, and that was just the first stop.

Planners didn't want the entire event to be just a passive viewing experience. They wanted people to have a chance to connect, especially with their new hires. The company had been growing so quickly during the pandemic that many people had never had a chance to meet their colleagues in person. As a result, event facilitators made a point of guiding participants through moments of social connection and team building. For example, at the snowy mountain retreat, there were Zoom breakout sessions. Everyone had been asked to create a virtual passport before the event, and the goal at this destination was to speak to as many people as possible and get them to stamp a page in your passport. It was a chance to "break the ice in the snowy mountains," von Alvensleben says.

It was the details that really made the event work. In addition to the props and backgrounds, everyone listened together as the MURAL band played music during a break. Anticipating the fact that some might have technical difficulties during the journey, the team created a #lost Slack channel that was monitored by a support crew. The event ended with everyone back together for a launch into space. "While cruising in outer space, we explored the idea of building a virtual MURAL Campus as we acknowledged that our distributed team will continue to work remotely for a long while as a result of the pandemic," wrote von Alvensleben. "Yes, our offices are still there but it's unlikely that we'll return to them any time soon. In the same way that tech giants succeeded in building their physical campuses that attracted great minds from all over the world, we imagined what it would be like to create our virtual space for MURAListas working from anywhere."

It was a truly unique event. Like we talked about in Step 4, MURAL CEO, Suarez-Battan, believes in learning through experimentation, or what he calls "smart experimentation" in that people need permission to try things out, see how they work, and then get better as they go. With their virtual retreat, he says, "Some things worked, some things didn't, but it was fun." And that was the main purpose: to celebrate what they had accomplished and to enjoy being together while they did it.

Since then MURAL has continued experimenting with these kinds of events, as have so many companies. We tell you this story, not so you get the impression that connection should only happen digitally—in fact, as you'll see in this chapter, we believe strongly in the critical role of bringing people together in person. MURAL's gathering was so successful, not because of *where* they held the event, but because of the intentionality they brought to planning the *why* and the *how*. If MURAL could do that with digital tools alone, think what you can do when you also have access to shared space that can be used for the purpose of building connection and belonging.

When Future Forum planned its 2021 offsite, for example, we focused on two things—planning our path forward and building relationships—and we did those things by designing a get-together that could accommodate both in-person and remote participants. The idea was to allow people to take part however and from wherever they chose. Instead of relying on a typical dinner or happy hour to build connection, we crafted a "team dynamics" session where we shared details about our personality types. We used those discussions to dive deep into what makes us tick: how we worked, what happens when we're under stress, and what we need from the team. We found a new level of connection, especially with several new members, not because we all showed up in the same place (our facilitator was attending virtually!) but because we used the time together to build a meaningful understanding of one other.

These examples serve as proof that there are a wider range of options than just showing up every day at the traditional corporate headquarters. In fact, if done right, flexible work can provide an opportunity to create a more connected and inclusive culture than ever before, and that's what we'll look at doing in this step.

The Importance of Connection and Belonging

To feel a sense of connection and belonging are basic human needs, regardless of what people do or where they live. From an evolutionary perspective, belonging to a group increases safety, and our brains are wired for it: Research suggests that a sense of belonging affects cognitive processes,[1] as well as physical and emotional health and well-being.[2] When people feel connected to something bigger than themselves, they are more satisfied and perform better at work, helping the organization achieve its goals.[3]

It's not surprising, then, that one of the most common concerns we hear about flexible work is that it will erode a company's culture and its employees' ability to connect with one another. Without a sense of connection and belonging, many executives fear that creativity, innovation, and collaboration will suffer. Forging a sense of connection and belonging is a legitimate concern for all the reasons we have touched on here, but the notion that needs to be challenged is this: Is gathering in an office really what forges those connections?

In fact, research suggests the opposite: **Flexible work is a critical tool in improving a sense of connection and belonging.**

In Future Forum surveys during the pandemic, when most employees were forced to be physically separate and work outside the office, we saw camaraderie actually *increase* among employees. Employees with time flexibility reported a greater sense of belonging (+36%) as well as an overall higher satisfaction with work (+50%). This was especially true for those in historically discriminated groups. Black employees in the US, in particular, have continued to see improvements in belonging quarter over quarter as organizations have settled into more flexible, distributed work. See Figure 5.1 which shows how sense of belonging at work has changed over time for different groups of people.

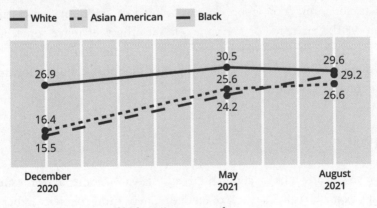

Figure 5.1 My sense of belonging at work

Source: Future Forum Pulse, 2021

As for the related concern that creativity and innovation will suffer if we're not together in the office, that, too, is a bit of conventional wisdom that isn't universally true. The reality is that where someone works has little bearing on how creative the team feels (see Figure 5.2).

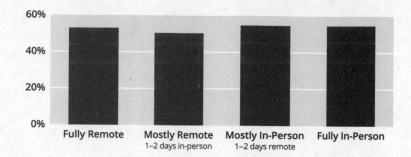

Figure 5.2 Percent of knowledge workers who agree that "my team is generating as many or more new ideas, products, services, or processes as we were in the past"

Source: Future Forum Creativity & Innovation study, 2021

What does have an impact on creativity is psychological safety: whether a person feels like their team is willing to take risks, and whether that person feels comfortable asking the team for help. Crucially, neither of those elements of psychological safety have anything to do with where people are located or whether they are working on flexible schedules.

What's more, the assumption that being in an office together builds our sense of connection ignores an important fact: Traditional office culture was never the right fit for everyone. Despite the preference some people have for it, office culture never really fostered connection and creativity for everyone in the same way. Consider some of the most common forums for connection in a traditional office space:

Meetings

As we've already talked about, meetings have become a real issue for employees at all levels. They too often drain energy and creativity rather than inspiring them, and interrupt people's ability to do important focused work. In addition, we almost surely all know someone, or have been someone, who has found meeting room dynamics challenging. It may be the introvert whose ideas and opinions get drowned out by louder voices in the room or, for that matter, on a video call. It may be the junior employee who is reluctant to speak up in front of senior colleagues. It may be someone who is new to the organization and hasn't yet found his or her footing. In many teams and departments, the same few voices tend to dominate and drive conversations, and not always because they have the best ideas and opinions.

Lunchrooms

Where to sit? Who to sit with? Should I sit alone or just bring food back to my desk? While eating together can be a great way to build relationships, for some—like new employees, shy people, or anyone who doesn't fit in easily with the prevailing demographics—it can be a context where they feel excluded, not connected. "It was so silly, but it felt like being back in high school and not in a good way," as one employee put it about having to navigate the social situation at lunch in her new company when she looked around and realized she was one of the few people of color in the room.

Happy Hours

For people who are less social, these kinds of gatherings, which are common at so many companies, can make them feel more awkward than connected. We know of one person who, as a recovering alcoholic, found the department's weekly beer chat to be something he dreaded each and every Thursday. A similar thing has happened with newly pregnant colleagues who have had to field questions they weren't yet ready to answer about why they weren't drinking during team dinners. A lot of people like these sorts of events, but quite a few people don't.

We don't make these points to suggest that you can never have these sorts of gatherings or that people need to be shielded at all times from any potential awkwardness or discomfort. We make them to ask the questions: When you plan such things, what makes you so sure they're actually building connection as they're intended to do? For whom are they building connection and at whose expense? Are we really so certain that they build connection in the way we think they do and that they build it for everybody equally? And, if not, might there be better ways—ones that are more likely to be effective *and* inclusive of more people, not just those who are louder, more extroverted, more senior, and more likely to fit in?

"Yes, gathering is about connection, but it's also about power," says Priya Parker, author of *The Art of the Gathering*. "Pretending power dynamics don't exist will make you a less artful gatherer."[4] As a leader, it's on you to deliberately design an environment that levels inequities and invites people to contribute.

Each of the forums listed above, from meeting to informal gathering, can be opportunities to build connection. Or, they can be instances where connection is undermined. The difference depends on the level of intention in which they are planned and executed. It's that intention that's most important—just like we saw with MURAL's detailed planning for their World Tour—not the forum in which the gathering takes place. Furthermore, while these may be the forums we're most used to, they are far from the only ones in which connection can be built.

Connection and belonging are important, to be sure, but if companies really believe these are essential elements of their culture, then they need much more than just office space to make sure that they are—they need a more fundamental redesign of not only physical space, but around all the ways in which connection can be built.

What Really Builds Connection

Despite what recent research shows, and despite the numerous ways in which office culture can make all kinds of people feel alienated, many people still feel like gathering in office spaces is the only way we can build real connection and belonging.

What we have found generally happens is that people—especially those who have been around for a while and have already succeeded in office culture—tend to default to offices because it's how things have always been done. They often do this without asking whether it was really better.

Part of the reluctance to let go of the idea that physical office space is *the place* to gather and do work stems from the fact that companies have invested so heavily in it, especially in recent years. In the US alone, nearly $500 billion is spent on office real estate transactions every year.[5] To attract top talent, many companies have spent a great deal of resources on highly decorated and tricked out office spaces (i.e. restaurants, fitness centers, lounges, game rooms, meditation centers, cafes) and in-office perks (i.e. child care, car washes, hairdressers, massages, happy hours, spa treatments) to try to ensure that people enjoy being in the office. The goal of making work life better for their employees is a good one, but we believe leaders can see flexible work as an opportunity to redirect some of those resources to be used in new and more advantageous ways.

Another big part of the reluctance has to do with people's inability to imagine an alternative. They've simply never seen it happen before, so how can they know it will work?

So, what does a connected workplace actually look like? And how can we take an honest and fresh look at how we're crafting truly connected experiences for our people—ones that invite everyone to participate and contribute no matter where, when, or how they're working. Because yes, it can be done.

The rest of this step is about what you can do to start building connection in new ways, ones that support flexible work *and* forge better, stronger bonds. We're going to talk you through several ways to build a connected, flexible workplace, which include:

- Acknowledge the challenge
- Look at what people actually want
- Make digital space your new headquarters
- Rethink the role of shared space
- Give teams the freedom to decide
- Support teams with options and tools
- Set the tone from the top

Acknowledge the Challenge

Bringing people together in a productive way is difficult (as the research on meeting fatigue suggests), and bringing them together in a way that builds connection (rather than undermine it and alienate certain groups) can be just as hard. Despite the common assumption that in-person is better, these things are challenging no matter what the forum. Throw flexibility into the mix, and you have something new to consider when sorting through this important challenge.

For example, Parker points to hybrid meetings, where people may not have equal ability to participate. "If I'm at home and my child is napping in another room and my colleagues are in the office chit-chatting and drinking coffee together before the meeting starts, that is an unequal power dynamic." The first step to leveling this inequity, says Parker, is simply to acknowledge it. "Hybrid gatherings aren't one gathering—they're three. There's the experience of the people in the room together. There's the virtual experience. And then there's the mix of those people interacting. You need to acknowledge that people are living in different realities."

You have to start there because being conscious of the realities is the only way to do something about them. One of the fringe benefits of moving to flexible work is that it requires us to disrupt old habits and behaviors that may never have worked as well as we thought they did. And once disrupted, we can move forward with more intentionality about what we want to replace them.

The following sections will provide further help, but in the toolkit at the back of this book, you will also find a tool, based on Parker's work, for Creating Meetings that Matter (page 193) that we recommend you use will also find a tool, based on Parker's work, that we recommend you use in planning any sort of gathering—big or small; digital, in-person, or hybrid.

Look at What People Actually Want

We've told you more than once now how much people want flexible work: 93% of knowledge workers want more flexibility in *when* they work and 76% want flexibility in *where* they work. But crucially, this does NOT mean that people never want to come together to connect in person.

Flexibility means having *choices,* and that includes choices about when, where, and how often to come together, as well as for what purposes. People want to be able to make these kinds of choices for themselves and with their teams, rather than just gathering at the office every morning at 9:00 a.m. as the default.

The data tells us that people still want the option of the office, but most don't want it for all aspects of work. Instead, most want it for the specific purpose of building relationships and making connections. Future Forum's research shows that for every person who wants office space for

For every 1 person who wants office space for quiet, focused work . . .

 4 people prefer using office space for **team or coworker interactions**, like collaborating, client meetings, and building camaraderie.

Figure 5.3

Source: Future Forum Pulse, 2021

quiet, focused work there are four people who want it for team or coworker collaboration and camaraderie (see Figure 5.3).

This is important to understand because too often people make the assumption that flexible work doesn't allow for in-person connection, but that's only true if companies decide to make it that way. The classic densely-packed, open floor plan workspace is part of the challenge that needs to be solved. The reality is Digital-First doesn't mean "never in person."

Even companies that have adopted Digital-First or "fully remote" strategies still consciously created ways to get their people together. GitLab, for example, is a fully remote company that plans in-person gatherings with the explicit intention of building social connection among team members. "We'll often get the question: 'As an all remote team, do you ever. . . see each other in person?'" says Darren Murph, Head of Remote at Gitlab. And the answer is a resounding yes. "It's vital to who we are."[6]

Once a year, in a different city around the world, the entire company gets together for what they call GitLab Contribute, which begins and ends with keynote addresses, and then "everything in between is optional excursions for people to get together and bond as humans and build relationships in person," Murph explains. They also have regional events throughout the year, as well as sales events, marketing events, and more. They know that without these events, their people might not see each other more than once or twice a year, if at all, so they're very intentional about planning them and enabling as many people to attend them as possible.

Zapier, another all-remote company, has taken a similar approach. Cofounder and CEO Wade Foster writes, "While we firmly believe that day-to-day work does not need to happen in person, we do believe that some things happen easier when in person."[7] It's the reason they get together for company retreats twice a year with the purpose of building connections and supporting the company's culture. "During the retreat, we do things that help foster our culture. Things like playing board games together and hiking as a group have helped us learn more about each other and our families—it's knowledge we wouldn't have gained in a normal week," Foster writes.[8]

When thinking about building connection in a flexible environment, it's important to remember that the office and offsites are still forums where that can happen. They just aren't the only forums.

Make Digital Your New Headquarters (and Give It the Same Intentionality)

If in-person gatherings are only one way to build connection, then what else can you do? As we've touched on in previous chapters, flexible work requires companies to reconceptualize the "workplace." It should no longer be thought of as merely a building, but as a network of equally important forums where work can take place and connections can be made. One of these forums could be a video conference, or a Slack project channel just as easily as it could be a conference room. It could be a shared collaborative document, like Google Docs, Quip, or Notion, just as easily as it could be an in-person gathering for a PowerPoint presentation. Communication can happen via communication platforms, emails, videoconference, chats, phone calls, huddles, direct messaging, social media, or in person. And people can engage in those communications from home, their car, while walking down the street, while sitting in a cafe, while traveling, or in an office building. The place and the method matter much less than the quality of interaction taking place.

Think about how much time was spent in the past on considerations about office real estate, decor, and seating assignments. Now, office space is just one dimension. Leaders instead need to focus on providing the forums and tools to support work and connection by whatever means and from whatever place makes the most sense for the people actually doing the work. That means thinking about digital with the same level of intentionality and investment as office space has gotten in the past. In fact, this switch in focus is overdue. Consider that during the pandemic, the office largely went away, and yet most knowledge work continued without significant disruption. But imagine if our digital tools and software went away. It's hard to imagine how work could continue without them.

The best way to break old habits and reconceptualize the workplace in this way is to make digital space your new headquarters. A digital HQ means that digital space, rather than a physical office building, is the primary place where people can access information, opportunity, and each other. The main benefit of that is that people can access those things no matter where or when they're working.

Making this shift means that leaders need to be intentional about the digital tools their company uses. For example, during the pandemic practically everyone learned that they could move most meetings to video conferences without sacrificing productivity. But we need to think beyond that to other ways of connecting virtually, depending on the task. MURAL, the company we highlighted in the opening to this step, offers virtual collaboration tools for brainstorming that can replace (and maybe even improve upon) the conference room whiteboard session. This book was written by the three of us using Google Docs, so we could co-create the work and share notes and research. Dedicated social channels for hobbies or interests can replace the break room chat. In MURAL's guide to facilitating remote workshops, which they created following their World Tour event, they advise looking first at the purpose of the event, not the forum in which it takes place: "When trying to employ a traditional method in a virtual session, look at the objective, and then be creative in how to get the same results with digital tools. In some cases, the Digital-First results can even provide better results than their traditional predecessors."[9]

New tools and technologies are being offered all the time, and keeping up is important, because employees increasingly expect it. In fact, digital investments can significantly impact employee experience: Employees who perceive their company to be an early adopter of technology reported scores twice as high for sense of belonging compared with those at organizations perceived to be late adopters, in addition to other benefits (see Figure 5.4).[10]

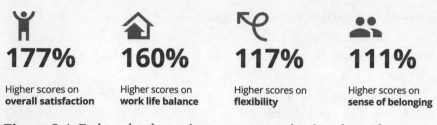

177%
Higher scores on
overall satisfaction

160%
Higher scores on
work life balance

117%
Higher scores on
flexibility

111%
Higher scores on
sense of belonging

Figure 5.4 Early technology adopters, versus technology laggards, across 4 dimensions of the work experience

Source: Future Forum Pulse, 2021

Some ways in which companies can promote the idea that digital is their new HQ include:

- **Use company-wide digital forums to build alignment:** Global communication channels can help anchor the organization around shared purpose and goals. Make them the primary place for communicating about the company's mission, vision, and priorities, and for sharing important metrics, news, and announcements.

- **Create a digital home for every team and project:** Project- and team-specific spaces make it easier for teams to collaborate. They should have spaces they can count on to share work, give feedback, access information, and connect with one another about their work.

- **Share online what happens offline:** Record as many meetings as possible and post videos or transcripts so everyone can access the information, regardless of whether they present. Make digital channels a repository for all-hands meeting recordings or leader presentation materials. This is a great way to build a common base of knowledge across your organization.

- **Create space to socialize:** Social channels can form around shared interests (like favorite TV shows, fitness groups, or hobbies). Host drop-in coffee breaks via video-conference. Headquarters is about more than just getting work done. It should also be a place to connect and build relationships.

- **Support Employee Resource Groups:** ERGs (LGBTQ+, Abilities, Women, Black, Hispanic/Latinx, etc.) have grown in importance for many people, and digital platforms allow groups to come together across geographies to meet and find allies.

Rethink the Role of Shared Space

None of us envision the office disappearing anytime soon, and because Digital-First doesn't mean "never in person," there's no reason why it should. In most companies it will still play a role. It just needs to be a different role, one that better facilitates flexible work.

Offices are too often densely-planned and generic because of dated assumptions that everyone needs an assigned desk, so buildings are filled with desks that sit empty much of the time. When offices are freed to be redesigned to support highly desirable experiences, it can completely shift how people think about space and help offices to be perceived as a benefit, not an obligation.

Recall the research earlier in this chapter, which told us that for every one person who wants office space for quiet, focused work, four people prefer using office space for team or coworker interactions. This means organizations need to think differently about how they utilize their space and prioritize areas where those interactions can take place. This doesn't mean that there should be no room for quiet work—remember, some people may not have home setups that are conducive to focused work, like those in small apartments or with full or noisy households. It just means a shift in emphasis.

"Each organization's balance of individual and team oriented areas should be driven by the nature of their work, but generally we're seeing a significant shift. Many offices were allocating roughly 80% of their floor area to assigned individual workstations and 20% to unassigned team collaboration spaces. That previous allocation and ownership model is evolving to 20% unassigned spaces for individual focus and 80% assigned spaces for team collaboration. This marks an evolution from individual desk-based planning to team-based neighborhoods which include both individual work points and collaborative spaces that are fine-tuned to the nature of work completed by each team. For instance, some teams may benefit from more open areas, while others really need a higher degree of enclosure."

— *Joseph White, Director of Design Strategy,*
MillerKnoll

Office spaces, in fact, can be designed to enhance connection and belonging. Research by MillerKnoll and Leesman shows that a sense of belonging among employees can increase by as much as five percentage points in thoughtfully designed spaces, like social commons that include some of the following elements:[11]

- **Perks:** Cultural touchstones like product prototypes or photos of employee events, as well as amenities like coffee and snacks can be a way to draw people in.

- **Choices:** Different areas and seating arrangements—like a comfy couch area versus a small cafe table and chairs—can give people options that suit different needs. They might gather to socialize or retreat to a nook for quieter, one-on-one conversations.

- **Vistas:** Open views increase the likelihood of chance encounters and encourage interaction.

- **Engagement:** Digital displays can provide a reason for people to gather for news updates or to digest timely content.

Other tactics that companies can consider include having separate floors or areas for quiet work versus social engagement, with the latter taking up more space because more people are looking for that option. Hoteling is another option, one that we use at Slack. When we switched to a flexible work model, we moved away from the traditional idea of the desk being each person's central point. We opted instead for hoteling for everyone— meaning instead of each person being assigned a desk, individuals or teams reserve desk space, conference rooms, or other such resources ahead of time as needed—because it supports flexibility.

What works best for your organization is obviously going to depend on the work that you do and the people who do it, but there are plenty of options available—ones that better enable both flexibility and connection. The greatest risk of all is when companies aren't intentional about how they use space and tools to support the culture they want.

Give Teams the Freedom to Decide (Because One-Size Does Not Fit All)

As we've seen with even all-remote companies, there is value in coming together in-person, but the frequency and cadence of those gatherings will vary greatly from team-to-team and organization-to-organization. Instead of focusing on top-down mandates—like how many days, or on which days, people should come into the office—organizations should allow teams to decide for themselves what works best.

A great way to guide teams in doing this is to revisit the TLA we introduced in Step 3, and use it as a tool for giving teams the freedom to do this within a framework. Remember that we advised you to start simple with your TLAs in order to make them easier to adopt, and then change or add as you go. This is a perfect opportunity to expand on them, and the topic can be discussed during one of the regular TLA check-ins that teams should have committed to already. Leaders can emphasize the most important elements in making this decision by framing the question that teams need to ask themselves. This isn't just about how often people feel like coming into the office. Instead, teams should be asking: What frequency and types of in-person interactions are required for us to operate effectively and build connection? Because it's important that teams do both.

For example, a Product Design and Engineering team might find value in coming together for a longer period (three-to-four days) each quarter to reconnect, talk product strategy, and plan their collective roadmap for the next quarter. Planning, especially for a large department, can be a complex and interconnected effort, making a longer offsite or onsite meeting highly valuable.

By contrast, a sales development or business development team is typically more regionally focused since sales organizations tend to map people to accounts within a territory. These teams might prefer to get together in-person two or three times a week to allow for day-to-day camaraderie (especially when they're getting rejected regularly on cold calls or outreaches), competition, and sharing of outreach strategies.

Each team should discuss the options and make the decision as a group. Team members should consider their collective function, circumstances, and the personalities of each individual in order to strike a balance. For example, some teams might be highly distributed in terms of location, so even if they enjoy socializing together, it might be impractical to get together in person more than once a month or quarter. In such cases, it can work better to intentionally spend the first few minutes of a meeting or weekly status update checking in personally with one another, or celebrate a product launch with a Zoom lunch where food is delivered to each person's home.

Other teams might be populated by people who have a lot of experience working together and deep personal relationships already built and may be less likely to need in-person gatherings to build a sense of belonging. A quarterly planning session might be sufficient. By contrast, a team with a lot of new employees might benefit from having informal get-togethers more often, at least in the beginning as they get to know one another—and then, because the work is flexible and adaptable, they can change their habits as their needs change.

What matters most is that team leaders refrain from making these decisions in a vacuum. Instead they need to have a high degree of self-awareness, as well as awareness of the personalities on their teams—a topic we'll talk more about in Step 6—so they can lead discussions and help teams come to an agreement that benefits them and the work.

Support Teams with Options and Tools

When giving teams freedom to decide their own norms and habits around gatherings, it's important for leaders to remember that, for teams to do this successfully, they will need operational support. For example, team leaders will need some training in how to bring people together in a way that fosters a sense of connection and belonging. So much of what makes a gathering successful, whether in-person or digital, comes down to the planning. Too often leaders convene a meeting without a lot of forethought (and we wonder why so many people feel like meetings waste their time). As MURAL CEO, Suarez-Battan, says, "It's really hard to run good meetings. We need to practice and be deliberate about the meeting." To do this, we suggest people start by asking themselves four questions before any kind of gathering:

- How can I be sure attendees will be comfortable and motivated?
- What's the topic and what do we need to achieve and produce?
- Who will facilitate the event and how?
- What tools will we need?

These were the same kinds of questions people at MURAL asked when creating their elaborate World Tour celebration, but they're equally important for smaller and more informal gatherings. Those last two questions point to another area where leaders need to think about how they can provide operational support. What forums are available for people to gather? How can you make it easier for managers to create intentional gatherings and honor their team's commitments? What will the travel and expense policy be for weekly, monthly, or quarterly in-person gatherings? In short, on a practical level, how will the details work?

Leaders need to be explicit about their policies around such things. Managers can be given a budget for planning events, for example, but that can put a burden on those who already shoulder so much. Instead of just having each frontline manager plan from scratch, one option is to give managers a menu of "pre-approved activity options" to choose from. That's something we're trying at Slack, and it allows managers to focus on the crucial *why* (the intention behind the gathering) and the *how* (how they will bring people together), rather than the logistics of it all.

Executives should also think about whether they need newly defined roles in the organization of people responsible for facilitating connection-building events and gatherings—whether in-person or virtual—just like many already have for facilitating travel. These are just some of the ways leaders can help ensure that a culture of connection is being built within the organization.

Set the Tone from the Top

"The two main tenets of the future are flexibility and connection," according to Levi Strauss & Co.'s Tracy Layney, and we agree. "So how do we lean into both of those things as we craft something for the future that's better than what we've had in the past?"

Your company's culture is vital here. It has to support these things or they will fail. As legendary management theorist, Peter Drucker, said, "Culture eats strategy for breakfast."

In our discussion of guardrails in Step 2, we talked about "leading by example" because the behavior of leadership shapes culture, even unintentionally. In fact, perhaps the greatest risk to a connected, flexible workplace is executive behavior. Companies that create policies that look flexible but allow executives to recentralize in one building, every day, risk creating a second class experience for those who are working more flexibly. The shift to this new way of working has to start at the top, but also engage people across the organization. Leaders need to be intentional about building an organization-wide culture that champions connection and belonging in a flexible work environment.

That means continuing to communicate about the advantages and expectations around a connected and flexible work strategy. If anything, leaders should err on the side of over-communicating, talking about this regularly and through all available communications channels in order to reach as many people as possible.

They also need to model the behavior, within their own teams, as well as more publicly. This is why at Slack we made a point of disassembling our C-Suite. No more corner offices and no more executive floor— perks that many top leaders see as symbols of their success—because in a flexible environment where people aren't coming into the office every day, we simply don't need them. This sent a signal to the entire organization about what's most important in our culture. And executives are still able to meet and communicate effectively even though the executive team is now distributed across multiple locations, including California, Colorado, New York, and even Australia.

On a personal level, there's plenty leaders can do to connect with team members no matter where they are. One of the most striking examples we've heard of this came from Indra Nooyi, former chairperson and CEO of PepsiCo. When she first became CEO, she went to visit her mother in India. One day her mother invited over friends and neighbors, and Nooyi got a chance to see person after person tell her mother how proud she should be and what a good job she had done as a parent. It was such a memorable experience that she decided to do something similar for her direct reports and their direct reports. She wrote a personal letter to each of their parents, essentially saying, "Thank you for the gift of your child to PepsiCo." They weren't form letters, either. She wrote specifically about how each individual had made a difference. Over the course of her career, Nooyi wrote about 400 of these letters, and it was a truly meaningful gesture for both team members and their families. One executive's father even made 100 copies of the letter, sat at the ground floor of his apartment building, and handed one to everyone who passed, saying, "I want you to see what the Chairman of PepsiCo thinks of my son."[12]

Nooyi didn't have to be in the same room with any of these people to build connection and make them feel valued. It's an example of the impact leaders can have when they get creative and are intentional in their actions.

"The first responsibility of a leader is to define reality," wrote Max De Pree, the late longtime CEO of Herman Miller (now MillerKnoll). We're living in a new reality, and we believe that leaders who work to foster feelings of social belonging and build connected organizations have the best chance at success. We will continue our discussion about the impact leaders can make in Step 6, as we talk about the new skills managers need for your flexible strategy to succeed.

Checklist for Step 5: Create a Culture of Connection from Anywhere

☑ Do you understand that Digital-First doesn't mean "never in person" and that a culture of connection is just as important—and just as do-able—as it was in office-centric cultures?

☑ Have you made Digital-First your new headquarters, the default place where people connect, collaborate, and get work done?

☑ Have you rethought how you can use physical space in new ways, ones that support connection and collaboration?

☑ Have you provided your people with the tools and resources they need to connect in a flexible work environment?

Step 6: Train Your Leaders to Make It Work: "Soft" Skills Matter More than Ever

The early 2020s will be remembered by many as the period when the nature of people management shifted. From the overnight move to virtual during the pandemic to the Great Resignation that followed, the shift from predictable, day-to-day management to continual discontinuity was taxing for managers. And it showed in their sentiment: our Future Forum global survey of knowledge workers found the following (see also Figure 6.1):

- Middle managers (defined as those managing 1–6 people) were 46% less satisfied with their jobs than senior managers (those managing at least 15 people).

- Managers struggled more than twice as much as executives when it comes to maintaining a sense of belonging.

- Managers felt more stressed and less productive than their more senior colleagues.

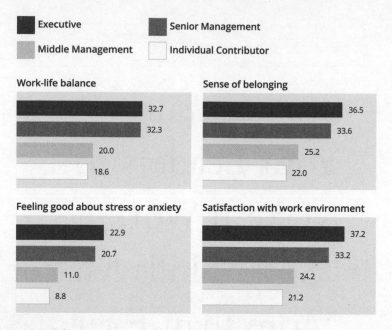

Figure 6.1 The employee experience of middle managers

Source: Future Forum Pulse, 2021

The Future Forum Pulse measures how knowledge workers feel about their working lives on a five-point scale (from "very poor" to "very good") across eight dimensions on a scale from −60 (most negative) to +60 (most positive).

And the disruption that caused these sentiments is likely to continue for some time. "No one knows anything for sure about what's coming," writes the futurist, Alex Steffen. "Being ready when the big shifts come. . . involves being able to work successfully in unprecedented situations." And that's the thing: People managers, by and large, weren't ready because they simply haven't been trained for this new way of working.

But some would argue that the shift in managerial roles simply revealed a problem that already existed. New challenges with flexible work made it harder for bad managers to go unnoticed, but many were already lacking the skills needed to lead complex teams of knowledge workers and their retraining should have started long before. More than a decade ago, Google started its Project Oxygen with the purpose of discovering what made someone a good manager, or if managers were even necessary for success. The results showed that not only did managers matter, but the best ones were, in fact, good coaches.[1] And yet, despite all the evidence about what it takes to be a great manager, research shows that most managers simply don't know (and weren't trained on) how to coach their people.[2]

Dawn Sharifan has been the Head of People at Slack since 2015, during which time she has led the organization through massive change, including rapid growth (both in revenue and people), a direct public offering in 2019, the pandemic and all its workplace fallout, a transition to a fully flexible work model, and an acquisition by Salesforce in 2021. She is viewed across the organization as the people-first leader who has spearheaded practices for inclusion and equity. She is also a certified coach who has long embraced the kind of coaching-first model of management that research shows is critical—not just for flexible work, but work in general. When it comes to her personal philosophy of management, Sharifan says there are three things that guide her:

First, "self-awareness is the key to everything." As a leader at any level, knowing your habits and triggers, knowing what you're motivated by, and trying to get a sense of your blindspots—these are the kinds of things that will allow you to lead and communicate with your team in the most effective way possible.

Second is to "have courage and be kind." Being in charge means making hard decisions, but you can always make them with empathy and awareness for those who are affected by your decisions.

Third is "clarity is kindness." People don't like to be in the dark, so clarity about what you're doing, clarity about why you're doing it, clarity about what you expect from people, these are kindnesses because they give people a sense of safety and predictability that allows them the freedom to do their best work.

"Those are the three things that guide me," Sharifan says. "I think there's sometimes a misconception that you can either be kind or you can be effective, but I believe you can be both. And I think you can be more effective if you're clear *and* kind *and* aware of your own B.S."

That philosophy laid the groundwork for Slack's Base Camp training for managers (and for much of the managerial philosophy you'll learn about in this chapter), which launched in 2018. Sharifan, and the team she led to build that training program, knew they wanted to help managers become the best leaders they could be, but they realized the company had never spelled out what "good management" looks like. So they started with the basics: They looked around the organization to find who among them were considered the best managers—the ones with the highest retention rates, the ones with the best reputations, the ones heading up teams that others asked to be transferred to, the ones who consistently helped their team members grow and take on new roles. Along the way Sharifan and her team made a point of consulting different voices from a variety of functions, levels, and demographics, as well as CEO Stewart Butterfield and a host of outside experts as the Base Camp program continued to evolve.

That program started before the pandemic hit and our offices shut down overnight. And it started before we decided to jettison our office-centric culture for a flexible work model intended to last well beyond the pandemic. None of this was an easy transition—far from it—but the emphasis on a coaching model and the skills our managers learned certainly helped. The company navigated all these disruptions without missing a beat.

Throughout this era of uncertainty, at least one workforce reality hasn't changed and is unlikely to change anytime soon: the critical role that managers play in your business and in the lives of your employees. But here's the harsh reality: Most of your managers are not equipped to embrace flexible working arrangements or lead distributed teams. Managers need to shift from gatekeepers who conduct status checks to coaches who lead with empathy. They need to get to know the people on their team, not just the skill sets to get the work done. In short, the role of a manager needs a new definition. This step will guide leaders in helping managers regain their footing and equip them for this new way of working.

Redefine the Role of Managers

You can seamlessly implement the first five steps, but none of these plans will scale or stick unless your managers are on board. That's because middle managers are the face of most organizations: They lead the people and they do the work. 56% of employees rate "my employer" as a very or extremely credible source of workplace information—and 77% say their employer is the institution they trust the most, above government, non-governmental organizations, and the media. But high trust comes with high stakes: 75% of workers cite a bad manager as the number one reason for leaving a job.[3] Researchers at Gallup cite a strong link between employee engagement and management quality, writing, "Performance fluctuates widely and unnecessarily in most companies, in no small part from the lack of consistency in how people are managed."[4] If you want to win the battle for talent, management training is not a challenge that executives can brush under the rug.

We have talked already in this book about how the conventional 9-to-5 working model has grown obsolete in today's knowledge economy. We have long known that digital tools have changed the way we work and communicate and that digital infrastructure is impacting the way we use physical office space. In the next and final step, we'll talk about how old expectations for managers to be clock-watchers and task-masters needs to change as well; they need to learn how to measure value based on outcomes, not individual activity or facetime.

With all these changes, it's time to get clear about what the role of managers should really look like today. Back in 1916, Henri Fayol described what he called "the Five Functions of Management," which included: planning, organizing, commanding, coordinating, and controlling.[5] For many, their conception of management hasn't evolved much since then. We would like to propose a new definition and purpose for managers to replace the old views. The role of today's manager is to do three things: **inspire trust**, **create clarity**, and **unlock the potential** within their teams (see Figure 6.2).

In practice this means:

1. Being transparent about the purpose, measurements, and expectations as a way to build trust.
2. Providing clarity for team members on their responsibilities and goals through direct (and two-way) feedback.
3. Unlocking potential for team members to do their best work through equitable practices and saying "no."

The following sections will look at the skills managers need to support this redefinition in any company, but especially one focused on flexible work.

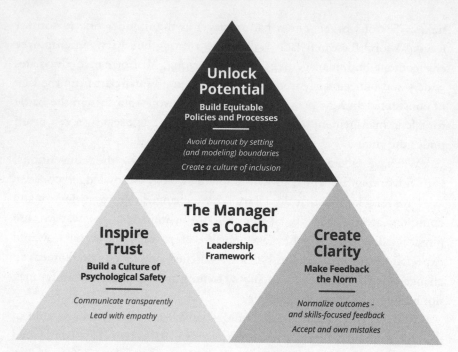

Figure 6.2

Adapted from Slack's Base Camp Leadership Principles.

> "It's really important to recognize that a manager's job is not to manage people. As a manager, you can manage process, you can manage time, you can manage resources. But you can't control people. . . And the more we try to control, paradoxically, the less effective we are in getting the outcomes we want. So as a manager, it's so important to think of ourselves as catalysts of great performance and ask ourselves, what can we do to be in service of bringing out the best in others?"
> — Tania Luna, co-founder of management training company, LifeLabs Learning[6]

Inspire Trust by Reskilling Managers to Create Psychological Safety

Harvard Business School professor, Amy Edmondson, defines psychological safety as "a belief that one will not be punished or humiliated for speaking up with ideas, questions, concerns, or mistakes."[7] The first step toward building psychological safety is to understand why it's so important in the first place. Psychological safety has been shown to be a prerequisite for high-performing teams, and if you can build an organization filled with high-performing teams, you will see benefits across the board. Companies with a high-degree of psychological safety are more likely to innovate, adapt to changes, and reap the benefits of diversity.[8]

Psychological safety is also the foundation of a "learning culture," one in which "people have the humility to know what they don't know and the curiosity to rethink the way they've always done things," writes organizational psychologist Adam Grant.[9] We just dedicated an entire chapter to learning and experimentation, so you know it's essential for flexible work. But even beyond that, learning cultures have long been shown to foster innovation and creative problem solving, while the old performance-oriented cultures often prioritize short-term results and time-tested processes over long-term growth and worthwhile risks.

Building psychological safety should be a core skill for any manager, but especially managers of flexible teams where employees are often engaged in new ways of working and collaborating that may be uncomfortable and unfamiliar. To help managers acquire this skill, reflect back on our advice for creating effective guardrails in Step 2: Executives have to lead by example. Psychological safety starts at the top, with executives developing and modeling the leadership behaviors they want to see across the organization, including: communicating transparently and leading with empathy.

Building Trust through Transparency

It's not just the day-to-day work that matters: leaders also need to inspire trust so that work gets done more effectively and efficiently. And trust doesn't happen without transparency—without people feeling like they understand what's happening and are respected enough to be informed. But based on Future Forum data, 66% of executives think they are being transparent, while only 42% of employees agree. There's that disconnect again that so often shows up between how executives and non-executives view what's happening within a company.

We've talked previously in this book about some of the ways you can build trust through transparency, like not waiting until you have all the answers before you communicate. Leaders at all levels can ensure transparency by being up front about what is known and what is unknown. It's often better to say "we don't have all the answers, but we're working on it" or "we're not ready to talk about this yet, but we know you're waiting and we will soon" than it is to say nothing at all. Because when you say nothing, you leave room for people to come up with their own narratives, as well as question your motives for keeping things from them that affects what they do.

Since communication is key to transparency, another important factor is to keep up with employee expectations around it—specifically around the channels you use and the frequency in which you use them. Once upon a time companies may have waited for weekly team check-ins or monthly department meetings to provide critical updates, but we live in a world where most of us are accustomed to being instantly updated about major life events via group text or social media. People have not only come to expect the same at work, these updates become vital for people to stay connected with "organizational buzz" when there are fewer opportunities to walk the hallways and overhear conversations at headquarters. "When companies don't keep up with new communication norms, the conversation doesn't stop—it just happens without you," writes Amanda Atkins, former head of Internal Communications for Slack.[10] Once again, it leaves room for people to project and wonder, and it deprives leaders of the chance to set the tone and direct the narrative.

Leading with Empathy

Empathy is such an important skill that IBM has a course on it that's offered on their internal learning platform. "During the pandemic, we trained 30,000 managers around this characteristic of empathy because we knew it was important," says Chief Human Resources Officer, Nickle LaMoreaux. It continues to be important as they implement their flexible work strategy, as it should be for all organizations.

There are a number of things you can do to help managers lead with empathy. As a first step, encourage them to facilitate a team discussion specifically about the mechanics and challenges of flexible work. Managers should lead the way by sharing how flexible work benefits them, as well as their own constraints and challenges, in order to model vulnerability and further build trust. Research shows that many people are reluctant to be the first to adopt flexible work practices, so it helps for managers to pave the way in order to legitimize the practices.[11]

Then, managers should listen to comments and concerns with an open mind. After all, it's easy to assume that your thoughts are how everybody else thinks, but that's often not the case. Remember the disconnect that we've been talking about and try to bridge the space between leaders and team members. Flexible work may be an already-established policy for your company, but that doesn't mean managers can't do their best to understand people's feelings about it and what their concerns might be. That's the first step in helping them see the potential for themselves, for one another, and for the organization.

A tangible tool managers can use to help build empathy is the "personal operating manual (POM)." POMs are documents that explain someone's personal communication style, preferences, pet peeves, flaws, aspirations, and other key bits of information about who they are and how they work. They complement the TLA (Team-Level Agreement) by providing a way each person can explicitly communicate to their team how they work, and what works best for them in a flexible environment. For example, in a section on "how to best communicate with me," individuals might write a version of the following statements:

- Content over format (and formality). I am a sponge. I like to receive content early, rather than wait for a formal presentation, and will always be glad to give feedback on early thinking.

- Bad news travels faster than good news. Please give me the bad news before I hear it from somewhere else. I would rather hear tough feedback directly.

- Audio-only where possible for meetings; video is just extra draining for me

- Be direct. Tell me what you need and when you need it.

Each individual team member creates one of these documents for themselves with the idea that they will be shared openly with the team. Then managers should lead a discussion about them. This practice helps coworkers see one another as people and sets the groundwork for interacting in a more compassionate and empathetic way. (You will find a POM template in the toolkit on page 198, along with instructions for filling it out.)

Just the act of creating a POM can help build the kind of self-awareness that Sharifan considers such an important management trait. Once again, managers should lead the way by being first to share their POMs to demonstrate vulnerability, letting team members know it's okay to bring their whole selves to the workplace, and encouraging team members to share their POMs with each other. One note of caution, however: this information should never serve as an excuse to make unreasonable demands. Just because you admit in your POM that you're "not a morning person" doesn't mean you get to snap at people in early meetings or expect not to be contacted before 10:00 a.m. on urgent matters. POMs are meant to help people better understand one another and navigate different personalities, but they aren't a license for bad behavior.

Levi Strauss & Co.: Lead with Empathy and Learn Together

A key principle of Levi Strauss & Co.'s flexible work strategy has been to "Lead with Empathy and Learn Together," which they communicated to their people this way:

> We will embrace clear communication and build a foundation of empathy as we learn and grow together.
> - Managers will need to lead with empathy and open-mindedness as they will be critical to successfully adopting these new ways of working.
> - Managers should be intentional in setting clear expectations for how their teams work together and how they deliver with excellence and a shared sense of community.
> - Managers, employees, and teams need to be in constant communication with each other.
> - We are on a journey together as we all create this new way of working. We will have patience and grace with one another as we learn, adapt, and grow.

Create Clarity

Managers need to know how to create clarity for their team members: People need to know what's expected of them and they need to know where they stand. This is always true, but it becomes *especially* important in a flexible work environment, when team members are working on different schedules and from different places, and when they are learning new behaviors and norms that are different from what they were used to.

Clarity also enhances the kind of psychological safety and trust that we just discussed. Sharifan likes to say (paraphrasing author and research professor, Brené Brown), "Clarity is kindness." It helps team members feel like they are on surer footing so they are free to focus on how to do their best work. In order to create clarity, managers need to know how to provide the right kind of feedback and own their own mistakes.

Offer Regular Feedback (But the Right Kind!)

Regular feedback sessions provide the most direct opportunities to connect with team members and provide clarity about goals and performance, but they should go beyond just check-ins and performance reviews. Managers need to stage regular career growth conversations and ensure that they are carving out time together across flexible schedules to talk through development. (Remember the 4D's: Development is one of the things that requires a live meeting—either in person or by videoconference.) Your best managers instinctively understand that the most valuable employees aren't motivated by money alone. They look for things like a sense of purpose, connection, and value. Managers need to be aware of the motivations— including career goals and aspirations—of their team members and assign roles and responsibilities to fit.

Lindsay McGregor and Neel Doshi, authors of *Primed to Perform*, describe this as "total motivation" (ToMo), which is defined by three direct motives: the play that people feel in their work, the purpose they find in it, and the potential they see for outcomes like career advancement.[12] As an executive, it's your responsibility to teach managers to stage regular, ongoing career-oriented conversations with direct reports. Not only does this demonstrate that they care, but it will also help them leverage the passions and interests of their team members and keep them connected to the team when working flexibly.

Managers need to be primed to accept feedback and direction, too. Each week during one-on-one sessions, Sharifan asks, "What's one thing I could be doing to make your life better this week?" Sometimes her team members just need to vent about something that's bothering them. Sometimes they need her to step in and speak to a colleague. Sometimes they need access to information or ideas on how to tackle a challenge. Whatever it is, the answer always gives her clarity into where people need help and how she can be more effective in unlocking their potential.

Managers also need to be self-aware about how they deliver feedback. For example, a few years ago, the Clayman Institute for Gender Research at Stanford analyzed hundreds of performance reviews from four different tech and professional services firms. The results were telling: Women were described as "supportive," "collaborative," and "helpful" nearly twice as often as men; women's reviews had more than twice the references to team accomplishments, rather than individual achievements; men also received three times as much feedback linked to specific business outcomes. The impact of this extends well beyond the individual review. When women ask for pay raises or promotions, they often experience backlash or punishment. It's a destructive cycle.

To be more equitable when providing real-time feedback or writing reviews, managers should ask each time whether they're focused on skills and outcomes, rather than prevailing norms of how work should be done or how certain groups of employees should act. It's an opportunity to check our own biases around facetime, for example. Do we believe an individual is performing better because of the impact or outcomes of their work? Or, is it because we see them more often in meetings or in-person? As we discussed in Step 2, being intentional about some of these inherent biases can help us create a more equitable and inclusive environment no matter where or when team members are working.

A few simple things everyone can change today:

- Celebrate individual achievements by focusing on the business impact.
- Focus on outcomes when giving feedback to reinforce what's important.
- Be cognizant of the words you use to promote what's important to your team.

Accept and Own Mistakes

Managers need to create a culture of acceptance around mistakes and make it clear to team members that they aren't the same as failing. Mistakes should be part of any feedback discussions, but managers need to be careful about how they approach them. As Stanford professor, David Kelley, put it: "If you keep making the same mistakes again and again, you aren't learning anything. If you keep making new and different mistakes, that means you are doing new things and learning new things." The latter is what you want to promote. In a learning culture, managers need to encourage people to learn and grow from their mistakes, which means striking a balance: Managers need to address mistakes and help team members analyze them to find the lessons, but they also need to avoid blaming people for not getting everything right the first time. (Of course, if they're getting the same things wrong over and over again, then that's a different story.)

Again, this is an area that bridges categories. It's something that managers need to be clear about, but that kind of clarity also enhances trust and psychological safety. In fact, accepting mistakes is so important to creating psychological safety that Edmonson includes it in her definition. That's because when people are afraid of making mistakes, it stifles creativity and innovation, and they're less willing to take risks—none of which are behaviors that lead to success in today's business world. As we all know, the backstory of any big business breakthrough, from Thomas Edison's lightbulb to Apple's handheld computers (remember the Apple Newton?), is filled with missteps along the way. And, as we discussed earlier, experimentation and openness to fail, learn, and iterate is required to help teams find the right flexible models for their needs.

Unlock Potential by Building Equity into Processes and Policies

The switch to a flexible work model requires an ongoing interrogation of processes and policies across your organization in order to unlock the potential of all your people. Leaders can do this by continuing to cultivate a learning mindset and asking questions like: Are our processes and policies fair and equitable? Have they been conceived for and by employees from diverse perspectives? Do they serve our goals for flexibility? Do they foster the success of underrepresented talent?

These are important questions because we often default to old habits and best practices, but such things were conceived to support systems as they used to be. Instead, Sharifan suggests "really getting curious about what this means—this program, this policy—*for our people right now*. Are we doing it just because it's easy and it's what we know how to do, or is there an opportunity to do things a different, better way?" In fact, designing with historically discriminated groups in mind often results in improvements that end up benefiting everyone. This phenomenon is known as the Curb-Cut Effect, a term coined by Angela Glover Blackwell, founder of PolicyLink.[13] The term takes its name from street corners where you find cutouts that make it easier for people in wheelchairs to cross. They exist, in fact, because of the disability advocates, but they have had the effect of benefitting just about everyone at some point in their lives—when they are pushing a stroller, hobbling on crutches, carrying weighty packages, or dragging a suitcase, to name just a few examples. As Blackwell writes, "Solutions designed to serve the most vulnerable lead to large-scale positive impacts."[14]

Bring All Your People In

Part of being a coach is modeling inclusive practices and resetting practices that create a culture of exclusion. Small talk can be a great way to add lightness to team meetings and check-ins and build connection, but managers need to be aware that too often the loudest speakers or biggest personalities dominate in such circumstances. There's also a danger that conversations can land on "exclusive" topics like summer homes, high-end restaurants, or inside-jokes that only include those in the know.

Managers need to be aware when leading such interactions. Consider how topics affect each person involved and then link conversations to team values, ask questions that all can answer, and make an effort to pull in those who tend to be quieter in group settings. Also think about a varied set of discussion formats, like audio-only, using the chat box, or submitting stories or ideas in advance where different formats might help different types of people chime in. All of these things can help foster psychological safety so that people are more comfortable speaking up and disagreeing because they are given paths to do so.

Provide Jump Balls for Talent

Burnout (which we'll talk more about in Step 7) is a danger of flexible work. But burnout is often cured when employees are excited about what they're doing and feel like they have the agency to deliver. In a more flexible work environment, managers become more important than ever as a connection point between people and different growth opportunities across the organization. Managers can build motivation by being proactive and providing more "jump balls" for employees. Rather than assign tasks, ask: "Here's an interesting opportunity, who wants it?"

When doing this, managers need to keep in mind that different people will respond in different ways, and then make sure opportunities are offered equitably across the organization. If they have an opportunity that may be perfect for someone who would otherwise not speak up to volunteer, they should proactively reach out and offer it. Make use of people's POMs to better understand what opportunities would excite them and how they might like those opportunities to be communicated to them. This tactic is a way to provide people with exciting, new challenges to drive both personal and professional growth for all members of the team.

Avoid Burnout by Reskilling Managers to Enable Boundaries

Trust, clarity, and potential are all undermined if team members are suffering from burnout. It's important that guardrails are put in place against it, and that managers are conscious of them because flexible work can have the effect of blurring boundaries. If you have schedule flexibility, you can choose when to do much of your work, but then how do you make sure that you, and your people, aren't working all the time? If you have location flexibility, you can WFH when you choose to, but then how do you know when to stop? Too often digital changes and flexibility have meant that the old hustle culture has been put on steroids. Leaders need to show how to build boundaries, which is about a lot more than just saying it's okay to have them.

Let's take focus time, for example: One of the main purposes of setting collaboration hours is to provide people with predictable times when they can count on getting focused work done without being interrupted by meetings or calls for help or feedback. If you think about it, it was once rare to book meetings back-to-back-to-back. If nothing else, you had to factor in travel time to another conference room, which might be on another floor or in a different building on campus. But with Zoom, it's far too easy to take one meeting after another without leaving your desk, which leaves too many people feeling overbooked, overwhelmed, and like the only time they can get focused work done is during "off hours" like evenings and weekends.

This kind of overload has become a big enough problem that some companies have started tracking it. During the pandemic, Uber tracked the use of collaboration tools like Zoom and Slack and found the following: 1) a 40% increase in meetings and a 45% increase in the average number of participants per meeting; and 2) a greater than threefold increase in Zoom meetings and Slack messages. These interactions resulted in a 30% decrease in focus time.[15]

According to the authors of "Collaboration Overload" in *Harvard Business Review*, which reported these findings, "These demands, which can be invisible to managers, are hurting organizations' efforts to become more agile and innovative. And they can lead to individual career derailment, burnout, and declines in physical and mental well-being."

One thing that companies can do is **call attention to the problem**. Even at an individual level, managers can be encouraged to talk with team members about the dangers and notice when someone might be falling into the trap. One of these benefits of today's digital tools is that you can tell when someone sends an email or posts on digital platforms. If a manager notices communications coming in at all hours and wonders when that person finds time to sleep, that's a good subject to bring up in their next one-on-one and ask whether the person could use some help.

Another thing that managers can do is practice good **presence management** with their teams. Professor Tsedal Neeley defines it this way:

"Presence management describes our digital presence, even where we don't share a space. We have to actively ensure that we are felt as present, even when we're not there."[16] This can be done in all sorts of ways—including through the messages people send, their status updates, and the way they participate in meetings—and it's an important topic to discuss when creating or updating TLAs. In a flexible work environment, people need to get into the habit of signaling when they're available and, just as importantly, when they're not because managers and colleagues can't simply walk by their desk to see. Sharing calendars is a great way to do this, as is agreeing on times when it's okay to turn off notifications.

Of course, presence management needs to be practiced in a healthy way so that people aren't made to feel like they need to show near-constant availability to prove their worth. At Slack we also promote the idea of setting healthy boundaries and taking time for oneself through the use of notifications that reflect more than just a person's presence at work. Someone engaged in focus time might use the writing emoji, while someone taking a break posts the dog walk emoji. Sharifan explains that, at Slack, "We've really tried to normalize what we call E.T.O., or emotional time off. We post E.T.O. to say 'I'm taking a mental health day because I just need a break.'" It's one of the tactics that sprung up specifically because of flexible work. "I don't think that would have happened if we were all still going into the office," she admits.

If boundaries are going to mean anything, managers also need to make clear that **it's okay to say "no."** Most people grapple with saying "no"— "no, I can't make that meeting," or "no, I don't have the bandwidth for a new project right now"—because they don't know they can without getting penalized, because they want to be helpful, or because of the dreaded FOMO. We've talked about how creating clarity is key to effective management. That also means helping team members feel comfortable sending clear messages to their manager and to each other about what they can and cannot do.

As always, leaders at all levels need to set an example, modeling these behaviors and normalizing them. Involve team members in discussions about setting productive boundaries and create clarity by using TLAs to spell out anything you decide that supports this goal.

Permission to Say "No"

There are specific steps we suggest to promote the idea that it's safe to say "no":

- **Prioritize:** Executives should establish a weekly habit of asking every single person on their team whether their workload is manageable. They should ask their managers to do the same with their own teams. Then canvas the company to find out the results. Both executives and managers should make it safe to say "no" by working with people to analyze what they're doing and offload things that don't matter.
- **Communicate:** Reinforce these priorities by saying what does matter and why. Explain what doesn't matter and why. Celebrate focus.
- **Decide:** You manage a team, and therefore you are the decision maker. Tell your team that you expect escalations from them. Escalate the things you cannot decide. If you don't know whether you're the decider, escalate that too.

Redesign Career Tracks

Reskilling managers to inspire trust, create clarity, and unlock potential will set managers up for success. In addition to that, leaders need to reevaluate who becomes a manager in the first place. Not everyone who currently holds the position will be well-suited for the kind of reskilling we've talked about here. Some won't have the necessary abilities while others simply won't like the idea of being a coach rather than a task-master.

This can mean that some people would be more likely to thrive on an individual contributor track, and companies should take this as an opportunity to redesign what career development can look like in a flexible work environment. In many organizations, the only way for people to advance is by becoming a manager, which leads to a large group of people in power positions, including some with no real desire to lead. To address this, a number of companies are creating multiple career tracks for people to advance within the organization: a management track and a non-management one. This has become a popular practice in the tech industry, with companies like Apple and Google offering a technical or expert career development track alongside a managerial one. Slack, for example, has an expert track where people can be promoted as high as the Vice President level, based only on their abilities and outcomes, without having to manage anyone at all.

There are lots of people out there who are both ambitious and talented, but not particularly interested in or good at managing people. Providing a non-management development track helps organizations retain these contributors while also ensuring that those who do become managers actually want to do the work.

Invest in Reskilling Your Managers to Inspire Trust, Create Clarity, and Unlock Potential

With flexible work and digital tools emerging as norms in business, leaders need to redefine the roles of their managers and train them to succeed in this new landscape. Otherwise, they will fail. Reskilling managers in this way requires continuous investment. "This is about building higher order management skills, like really leaning into listening and empathy," Levi Strauss & Co. Chief Human Resource Officer, Tracy Layney, explains. "I think that's going to challenge a lot of companies because I don't think that we've always given these things that level of investment."

Three things that leaders can do for their managers to make this shift and enable flexible work are to:

- **Invest in coaching:** At Slack every one of our managers gets a coach from the get-go, and not just when they've made a mistake or are in danger of losing their jobs.

- **Invest in structured feedback:** Every manager leaves our Base Camp training with an "accountability partner" so they can help keep one another on track and ensure that this isn't just another corporate training that's soon forgotten.

- **Find ways to celebrate great managers:** This is the best way to market your priorities and drive the kind of changes you're looking for.

Our Base Camp program has been popular among our people, with many people managers reporting they have been grateful for the guidance.

The one part of it that they consistently praise the most is how it creates a "community of managers." Through the program, managers get a chance to talk with one another about the challenges they're facing. "Management can feel very isolating," Sharifan explains, "so by providing a forum where they can be vulnerable and honest, and say to their colleagues, 'I'm dealing with this really hard issue with one of my employees' or 'I'm just stuck on this problem and don't know what to do next,' it has been such a valuable experience for them." Organizations that are successful in transitioning to flexible work will focus on providing managers with the support they need so they don't feel like they're going it alone.

As you think about investing in your managers, you may be asking the question: "How will I even know if this is working?" Measuring outcomes over activity is key for both organizations and managers. In the final step, we'll talk about how to actually measure what's going well and what's not as you implement these steps in your organization.

Checklist for Step 6: Train Your Leaders to Make It Work

☑ Do you understand the new role managers play in today's workplace, and especially in a flexible workplace?

☑ Have you communicated with your managers about the new skills you want them to develop, like inspiring trust, creating clarity, and unlocking potential in their team members?

☑ Are you leading by example and modeling the behaviors you want managers to adopt and encouraging them to do the same with their teams?

☑ Are you ready to invest in new training and resources for your managers to help unlock their potential?

☑ Have you provided opportunities to grow for those who don't want to manage?

Step 7: Focus on the Outcomes: Avoid the Doom Loop and Embrace the Boom Loop

"How will we know if people are really working?"

It's an all-too-common question that comes up about flexible work. Executives, managers, and even some employees wonder how to tell if team members are actually doing their work if you can't just look over at them to see.

One software company executive developed a standard answer to this question: "How did you know they were working when they were in the office?"

Attendance. Hours logged. Speed of response. These are some of the things that leaders have looked at in the past to measure individual performance. But in a flexible work environment, they simply don't work. (In fact, there's good evidence to suggest they never really worked that well—a subject we'll tackle in this step.) Companies that are successful in adopting flexible work strategies are also implementing new strategies for measuring how it's working.

At Boston Consulting Group (BCG), people tend to work on dynamic teams that frequently shift in composition, which can make measuring team success difficult. Still, Managing Director and Senior Partner, Debbie Lovich, says that for them, it comes down to asking: "Is the team delivering value to the client?... and are they delivering that value in a skill-building, rewarding, and sustainable way?—with the latter measured by cultural factors that promote predictability, learning, recognition, and psychological safety."

The focus on learning, sense of accomplishment, and sustainability can seem somewhat unexpected for a professional services firm where client needs often trump everything else. Even so, BCG has found that their success lies in delivering value for and with their clients, of course, but also in knowing that they are doing so in ways that engage, energize, and support the people charged with providing that value. To drive employee engagement as a key outcome, Lovich led the creation of a global program called PTO (predictability, teaming, and open communication), aimed at ensuring a positive employee experience by prioritizing three key things:

- **Predictability:** Protected time each week for every team member to go truly offline, and, more importantly, learn how to go offline without stress.

- **Teaming:** Collaborating as a team to make sure every person gets their time off, as well as establishing clear team norms to make the unspoken spoken—including specifics about things like when the start and end of day are, expectations for off-hour work and communications, travel expectations, response times, preferred modes of working, etc.

- **Open Communication:** Regular, coach-facilitated team conversations to resolve issues early. The coach also has one-on-one sessions with team members to make sure all issues get surfaced in a productive and constructive manner.

The impetus for creating the PTO program was a chance call Lovich got from a friend asking for a favor: This friend knew an academic named Leslie Perlow who was looking to research the way consultants did what they did and whether there were better ways of working. Perlow needed access to consultants for her research and wondered if BCG might open their doors to her and her team.

The call happened to come around the same time that Lovich and her husband were having some frank discussions about how their lives worked. The couple had four kids and lived in Boston, but Lovich commuted each week to a long-term client of hers in New York. She would leave at 6:00 a.m. Monday mornings and not return until Thursday nights, often after the kids had already gone to bed. Lovich's husband pointed out that if she were considering taking a new job under these conditions, they would have a serious talk about whether this was the lifestyle they wanted, but since Lovich had worked for BCG for over a decade—starting before they had children—they had never had that conversation. The request to do research with BCG came exactly when Lovich realized she needed to look more closely at her own work life and whether there was a better way of doing things, so she got the okay from the company to let the researchers in to examine how they worked.

It was a several-year process before the research eventually developed into their PTO program, but during that time researchers found that one of the main things that frustrated employees at BCG was a lack of predictability. Employees knew what they were getting into when they joined the consulting business, and they expected to work hard and work often. They knew work would entail some late nights and some weekends. What bothered BCG employees was the lack of predictability in when those would be, and that they couldn't predict with confidence when they would get time off for themselves—to spend with friends and family, to get personal stuff done, to rest, or to just have a predictable life outside of work. So the researchers suggested they test the idea of instituting a mandatory evening off each week. (That may not sound like a lot, but in the always-on culture of consulting, it was a big shift.) The team would agree on the timing together, and then everyone could count on having that time to themselves.

Out of that grew the need to have facilitators (or what they now call PTO coaches) to help support teams in this, so that they could agree on boundaries and stick to them. (There was, in fact, some "cheating" early on where people would still try to bring work home to do on their nights off.) But as soon as these kinds of fairly straightforward changes took hold, employees were reporting that they were happier, more productive, and learning more. On top of that, Lovich's upward feedback scores—which she admits had been pretty average up until that point—shot way up. In the meantime, she also decided to give up her New York clients and start building a client base in the Boston area so she could have more predictability in her own life as well.

In order to roll out these ideas to more and more teams, the formal PTO program was created. It focuses on measuring and improving team experience *during* a project, when leaders still have a chance to fix problems and make improvements, instead of waiting until after a project is finished to survey members. Those measurements are shared in a weekly team dashboard that makes the results plain: results are plotted on a spectrum from positive (green or "Good intensity" zone) experience to negative (red or "Grind" zone). "If the case team dashboard is red, then we know we need to start stepping through some interventions," says Lovich. "PTO helps us not have to wait weeks or months to make the experience better for our case teams (see Figure 7.1)."

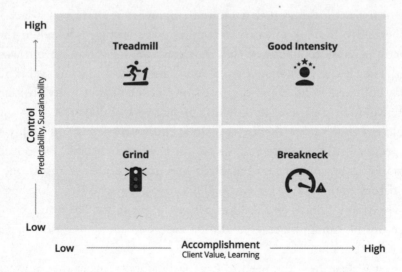

Figure 7.1

Source: Boston Consulting Group

Employee experience is an important measure because it can be tracked in real time and because of its link to better business outcomes. For BCG, their commitment to better ways of working has certainly helped them win the battle for talent: Lovich cites it as a key factor in their longstanding ranking by *Fortune* as one of the top companies to work for.

For every leader who asks, "How will we know if flexible work is working?", there are good answers, and in fact, better answers than they likely had when their teams were working in the office. There are ways to lead teams and companies that result in both happier, more engaged employees *and* better outcomes for your business. But getting there, as you will see in this step, isn't just about dashboards of metrics, though those are important. It's also about understanding and articulating your most important goals, being clear about priorities, and investing as much in understanding employee engagement as business outcomes.

What's Wrong with the Old Way?

Flexible work presents an opportunity to measure progress and success in a better way, but before getting into that, we want to talk about why some of the old ways should be abandoned.

With flexible work, it's not possible to measure individual productivity in the same way that many companies have in the past. You can't clock when someone shows up at the office. You can't "manage by walking around" to check what people are doing. You can't note how late someone stays at their desk. But the truth is this: these old activity-based measures that were developed in a bygone era have long been ineffective for knowledge work that tends to be more complex, creative, and not easily measured in the same way—so it's past time that we get rid of them anyway.

It comes back to that software executive's answer to the questions he often gets about employee productivity in a flexible work environment: "How did you know they were working when they were in the office?" Were we ever really able to know that employees were being productive just because we saw them sitting at their computers or present in the office? The answer, quite simply, is no. They could be messaging with friends, shopping online, researching camps for their kids, checking their dating apps, chatting with colleagues, reading the newspaper online, or so many other things that have nothing to do with getting work done, let alone getting *quality* work done. As one senior media company executive admitted to us: "I guarantee you I spent a lot of hours in the office in my twenties, and I wasn't working most of those hours."

The traditional, over-the-shoulder monitoring methods were always flawed, especially when trying to apply them to today's knowledge work, which is increasingly complex and uncertain. The rise of flexible work just makes them even more inapplicable. Flexible work demands that we move away from activity-based measures (hours worked, keystrokes logged, laptop hours, presenteeism) and to outcomes-based ones (results delivered)— which is a better measure anyway. After all, do you really care about the *quantity* of hours someone works or the *quality* of the work they get done? More deeply, this means we need to move to setting goals and coaching teams to meet them instead of monitoring to ensure "work is being done."

Abandon the "Monitoring" Mentality

Flexible work arrangements have a tendency to bring to the surface common challenges around trust, which was, as you will recall, a key topic in Step 6 about reskilling your managers. Some leaders feel like they won't be able to know if their teams are working if they're not in the office or if they're unable to monitor that they're online. "If I can't see them, how do I know they're working" is an idea ingrained in so many of us, and not just leaders.

Heidi Gardner and Mark Mortenson wrote in the *Harvard Business Review* about a regional bank where in-office employees would submit anonymous questions at the weekly all-staff town hall about whether their co-workers at home were "actually working." As the authors wrote:

> "Each week, the president assures his employees that the business is on track and that measures of productivity (like the number of loans taken out) are above expectations. "But it's exasperating," he said. "No matter how much I try to convince them or even use numbers and other kinds of evidence, it's not sinking in. You'd think that if I can trust people, surely they can trust each other, right? But no.""[1]

This company had a trust problem. As a result of widespread distrust, some firms resort to monitoring. The issue with monitoring, however, is that it's ineffective at best; at worst, using monitoring to close the trust gap more often has the effect of further undermining trust.

First, monitoring doesn't work because there are always ways around monitoring systems. Just like how an employee can surf social media at their desk while keeping a work window open for when the boss comes around, so can employees find ways around time tracking or work tracking tools if they feel motivated to do so. There are also gaps in monitoring systems. You may be able to tell when someone is working, but that tells you little about whether they are working efficiently, effectively, or producing quality results. To give just one example of this, Brian's son did a college internship at a government institution where he was directed to keep a specific tool open for a minimum of 10 hours each week. Even though he could complete his work in less than three hours, and it was typically error-free, if he didn't log 10 hours his supervisors were afraid they wouldn't be able to justify that he was working hard enough. So he did as he was told. Monitoring most often encourages people to perform to the measure (i.e. keep my laptop open 10-plus hours a day), not to meet outcomes.

Beyond that, research shows that monitoring actually makes things worse. Trust is not built through surveillance, so monitoring only compounds the trust issues that inspire their use in the first place. It also hinders performance, negatively impacting employee satisfaction and overall morale, as well as contributing to burnout. One study found that nearly 50% of strictly monitored workers reported severe anxiety compared to only 7% of those without much monitoring.[2]

Leaders at all levels who try monitoring tactics run the risk of getting caught up in what we call The Doom Loop: an unhappy cycle of *monitoring*, which leads to *meaningless metrics* and time wasted on reporting, which leads to effort wasted on checking the boxes or *avoidance* of the monitoring systems, which leads to talent attrition, which compounds a *loss of trust*, which tend to lead to more *monitoring*. And on and on it spirals (see Figure 7.2).

A major problem with old systems of measuring and monitoring activity is that they try to oversimplify the answer to a much more complex question: how to effectively measure knowledge work. As an executive at a financial services company put it: "I keep getting asked for better productivity metrics. A lot of our executives don't trust people—but we've also come to believe that just because everything is now digitized that we can measure everything. But measuring the hours put into a new marketing creative, or how well someone closes the books, isn't simple." It never has

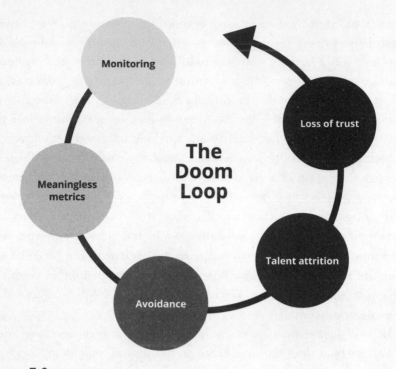

Figure 7.2

Source: Future Forum

been simple, and that's been true since long before most companies began contemplating the concept of flexible work.

Adopt a Better Way: Outcomes Over Activity

Winning the battle for talent requires a shift to flexibility. Getting the most out of that talent requires leaders to create clarity, inspire trust, and unlock potential, as we talked about in Step 6. But none of this will work if companies are still focused on measuring the wrong things.

Instead, organizations must focus on *outcomes* over activity. That activity is sometimes described as inputs (i.e. number of hours put in at the office) or outputs (i.e. number of bugs closed, events hosted, or social media posts produced). Your success as a company isn't measured in activity or effort put in, but in results. Why not manage your teams the same way?

So what does it mean exactly to measure outcomes over activity? As Dominic Price, "work futurist" at software company Atlassian, points out, "The way we think about productivity is based on a 250-year-old construct." Once upon a time, technological advances like mechanized farm and factory equipment led to daily output increasing considerably, and without the need for additional hours put in by workers. The old measures (i.e. bushels of wheat harvested or the number of steel beams produced per day) made a lot of sense in the Industrial Age, but far less so in today's knowledge economy. As Price notes, "Productivity has always been a good way to measure the impact of machines and capital. It's just never been a good way to measure the impact of *humans*."[3]

For example, suppose a manager has set a goal for her team of sales associates to make 40 calls a week (activity-based measure) to potential new customers. Team members will surely adjust their behavior to meet that target, even if it means spending less time with customers who are more likely to result in sales, or even with potentially high-value customers who might be willing to spend more. That target emphasizes the wrong thing, because what's most important to your company is whether the team is generating, not the amount of effort spent on calls. This kind of activity-based measure also takes away people's power to figure out what they need to do to make *actual sales*—not just sales calls. Does it really matter to your business whether it took 40 short calls or one long one to get there? Actual sales figures are a far better measure of individual performance, just as they are for your business as a whole.

To give another example, Price talks about a marketing manager setting a target of publishing five blog posts a week. Once again, the marketer assigned this target will surely adjust her behavior to meet it. But even if met, does the target tell you anything about the quality of those posts or their effectiveness in reaching customers? No. What it does is force that marketer to focus on the wrong things, on quantity over quality. It also inhibits her ability to act in creative and innovative ways to produce results. A better, outcome-based target would be to challenge that marketer to increase traffic by 5% and then give her the freedom to experiment and figure out how to get there.

This kind of reorientation is something that needs to happen at all levels of your organizations. Leaders need to shift from monitoring activity (inputs and outputs) to a more holistic, outcomes-based approach. Quantity should never triumph over quality. Success requires clear goals set at both the company and the team level. This is important, not just to meet business outcomes, but also to foster the kind of culture you want to build—the kind that will help you win the war for talent.

Measuring Outcomes on Individual and Team Levels: Moving from Doom to Boom

It's through this kind of reorientation that companies can avoid The Doom Loop. Instead, trust gets built by being clear about shared goals and giving people the support and room they need to meet them. We call this The Boom Loop (see Figure 7.3 below).

For many leaders at all levels, managing to outcomes will be a new skill, which means developing new habits followed by lots of practice and reinforcement. This goes back to the new definition of management that

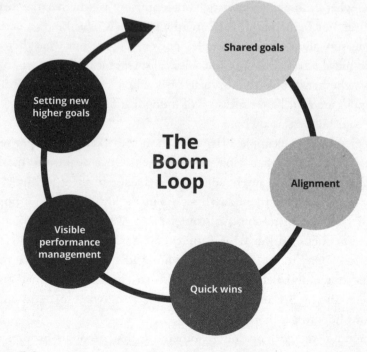

Figure 7.3
Source: Future Forum

we talked about in the last chapter. The key roles of managers—and, in fact, leaders of all levels—is to build trust, create clarity, and unlock potential as outlined in Step 6. In this context that means figuring out which outcomes matter, how those translate into deliverables, and how to set expectations to timeframe and quality. In other words, people need to understand what's expected of them (clarity), they need to believe that their work is being measured fairly (trust), and they need freedom within these clearly articulated parameters to do their best work (unlock potential). These things are essential for driving outcomes-based measures. They, in turn, rely on clarity from the top: clear articulation of purpose and goals and the prioritization of those things.

So what do managers need to do exactly to unleash The Boom Loop and move from activity-based to outcome-based measures?

For employees at the individual contributor level, managers need to:

- **Start with onboarding:** For example, at Slack we provide clarity for new employees by creating 30-, 60-, and 90-day plans that articulate expectations of deliverables and also drive learning.

- **Provide clarity on roles and responsibilities:** Ensure people understand their roles relative to others on their teams, and in the context of cross-functional projects. Are they responsible (versus consulted or informed), and if so, are their goals clear in terms of deliverables and timelines?

- **Conduct weekly one-on-ones:** Review priorities and commitments and make it easy to intervene when progress is lagging. (This is also a prime opportunity for managers to help team members set necessary boundaries, as we talked about in Step 6, encouraging them to speak up when overloaded and escalate issues that are beyond their ability to resolve—which will lead to better outcomes.)

At the team level, they need to:

- **Establish clear team goals and priorities:** Team goals should ladder up to overall company goals, and should have a longer duration—i.e. quarterly or half-yearly—with ways to track progress. Priorities need to be clear and cut across the team. They also need to be updated often enough to be responsive to changing conditions (typically monthly or quarterly), but not so frequently that they whipsaw teams and impact the quality of work.

- **Provide methods for communicating progress and updating status:** This needs to be done transparently and in a shared space to build trust. Collecting status asynchronously, on a standard schedule, and in a common tool helps managers understand what's going on within and across teams without adding yet another meeting to calendars. Sharing everyone's status in a public forum helps build trust and transparency within the team because it allows team members to feel engaged, know that others are also moving work forward, and find ways to get help when blocked.

- **Build continuous learning into team norms:** Weave into weekly team meetings a "team norms" check-in on a rotating set of topics (the aspects of your TLAs, for example). Hold "blameless retrospectives"— postmortem assessments that focus on what was done well and opportunities for improvement, but not on who to blame for hiccups— for all major projects (eg., the big quarterly release) and share the results publicly.

Leaders need to provide clarity around goals and transparently track progress on team projects, and one way they can do that is through the use of a responsibility assignment chart called the RACI matrix.[4] Each letter of the name stands for an element of the chart that makes clear who is Responsible (who does the work), who is Accountable (who assigns and signs off on the work), who needs to be Consulted (who provides input), and who needs to be kept Informed (who needs to be updated on progress and decisions). This method ensures that everyone in the group knows how to drive the work forward as individuals and as a team.

Continually Reassess Your Measures

It can take time to make this kind of switch in what you measure. Besides the experiments around flexible work we talked about in Step 4, measurement is an area where leaders need to experiment and learn as well, and make adjustments as they find what works.

At the start of the pandemic, for example, our engineering leaders at Slack were concerned about whether people could be as productive when working virtually as they had been in the office. Chief Technology Officer, Cal Henderson, admits he was skeptical. Initially, leaders determined metrics that were focused on two areas: 1) Jira tickets closed, and 2) surveys of individuals and managers. Jira is a tool used by engineering teams to track elements of work that need to be done, so a "closed" Jira ticket is essentially an activity-based measure. In the first weeks of the pandemic, Jira ticket closures actually grew. That should have indicated that productivity was soaring and the company was in great shape, right? Well, not exactly. It didn't tell you what type of tickets were being closed. They could have been small tickets for low-level tasks that would have minimal impact on the product vs. more complex and important work. So the team adjusted the metrics it measured, to look at better indicators of how teams, not individuals, were working: What could the tools they use tell managers about where teams were getting "stuck" in the process? At the same time, based on conversations with their team members, managers were expressing concerns that many of their people were struggling even if the metrics weren't showing it.

After that the engineering team shifted to emphasizing their surveys to measure how people were doing, and, when found to be struggling, what would help. This enabled them to address very specific issues—like inadequate home setups, better access to key tools and information, and help with prioritizing tasks—that would drive sustainable results. At the same time, engineering leadership started looking at different metrics that focused on long-term success. Around new product development, for example, they tracked not just what products they were launching, but also quality measures (how many bugs were being reported) and usage statistics (how quickly was the product being adopted). While not as obvious and immediate as tracking Jira ticket closures, looking at metrics tied to quality and growth gave them a far stronger indication of results.

It's important to note that for some functions, it's still possible to have quantifiable, activity-based goals for individuals as well as teams (though, as we'll talk more about in the next section, these should never be your only measures). For example:

- For customer support specialists, measurements might be tracked around first-time resolves, cases solved, and customer satisfaction.
- For engineers, velocity and quality metrics can be used, along with measurements of product usage.
- For sales professionals, revenue generation, renewal rates, and net revenue retained can be tracked.

For so many roles, however, assessment of both individual and team contributions involves balancing quantitative goals with qualitative ones like quality and timeliness. That requires some "judgement" from leaders, which can feel like an ambiguous word. The potential for ambiguity is why it's so important to be as clear as possible about measures of quality by doing things like sharing examples of what "good" looks like, talking about the level of collaboration you expect across a team, and setting goals around timelines for delivery. By making quality less ambiguous, you reduce the potential for biased judgement.

Getting to that level of clarity can be difficult for many managers and executives. It can even drive some to fall back on easily measured metrics, like hours worked or speed of response. This is why we spent time in the beginning of this step examining why those easier metrics and methods are largely ineffective, and in some cases even counterproductive and undermining. So, if you find yourself, or one of your managers, defaulting to old ways, the first step is to remind yourself of the downsides of that approach.

Next, leaders need to be encouraged to take some time to really look at this issue. In most organizations, the job of manager is much harder than it was a decade ago for reasons we've already mentioned, but also because many of the people reporting to them spend time working in complex, cross-functional workstreams. As a result, instead of focusing on managing only the function, leaders need to make sure that teams are interacting in healthy ways to meet goals while also building good habits and practices. The specifics about what works and what doesn't when tracking outcomes is ultimately going to be highly dependent on the person, position, team, and goals of the company in question, but it is the role of leaders in today's workplace (flexible or not) to sort through this, and then to communicate clearly about it with their team members. Executives can support this by removing pressure to get it all right the first time (remember the importance of "accepting mistakes" from Step 6), and instead encouraging managers to check in regularly and be willing to learn and adjust when things don't go to plan, much like our engineering team did during the pandemic.

Despite the complex environments in which many of us work today, there are still key measures that all leaders can rely on, quantifiable things that are consistent drivers of long-term performance, like employee engagement, which should be looked at no matter what function or company you're in.

Building Company Success = Business + People

Success in business is something that we're used to measuring. The famed Fortune 500 list ranks companies by the straightforward measure of total revenues. The Inc. 5000 list looks at the fastest-growing companies in America. These measures, however, tell you nothing about how these companies got there. In fact, "success" is a broad term that, in a newly flexible environment, needs to encompass both business outcomes—like revenue growth and profitability—along with drivers of long term performance, like employee engagement and customer satisfaction.

In other words, success is about much more than productivity alone. As we talked about earlier, success at BCG is measured in terms of both the value they deliver to the client and to their own people when it comes to them feeling engaged, rewarded, and like they are building their skills while working in a sustainable way. BCG tracks typical business performance metrics, of course—like revenue growth, recruiting, and retention—but those are lagging indicators. They don't tell you if you're on the right track today; only if you were on the right track last year. As part of their PTO program, BCG tracks the things that give them a better real-time status report. They do either a weekly or biweekly survey of each team on a few key success metrics, such as:

- Are we delivering value for our clients?
- Are we working efficiently?
- Does our team love working here?
- Is the work sustainable?
- Are we learning and developing?

The questions have to do with company culture as well as with the individual's sense of accomplishment and value to the organization, their ability to learn and develop, and the degree of psychological safety they feel with their managers and team members. These things are just as important to measure as profits because, as BCG found, companies with highly engaged workforces financially outperform ones without. In short, engagement is what drives those business incomes.

This is why companies need to focus on employee engagement as a key outcome. Research shows that companies with high levels of engagement outperform those with low engagement.[5] Higher employee engagement leads to higher margins, profits, and revenues,[6] as well as increased retention and customer satisfaction.[7]

At Dropbox, as they embarked on the massive shift to a flexible work strategy, they were inspired to "spend a lot of time . . . looking at performance based on results, not 'busyness,'" says Chief People Officer, Melanie Collins. In the process, the company broadened the key outcomes it measures to include both the impact on the business *and* on their people:

1. Business results: Are we performing as a company and meeting our financial goals (revenue, bottom line)?
2. Progress against our product roadmap: Are we accelerating our company mission with new features that support distributed teams?
3. Talent: Are we becoming more distributed as an organization (both through hiring and relocation)? Are we becoming more diverse as an organization?
4. Adoption: Are we adopting new ways of working? Are our people using the virtual tools and technology we're providing? Are they making core collaboration hours work and making use of Dropbox studios?
5. Employee engagement: Are we building virtual-first community and belonging? Are we shifting from office-centric to flexibility-centric? Are employees part of this change vs. having the change happen to them?

We talked earlier in this book about the success Dropbox has seen as a result of their shift to flexible work: a threefold increase in applicants, a 15% faster time to hire, and a 16% increase in diverse candidates.

Metrics around hiring (time to hire, hitting diversity goals), retention, and rates of promotions across groups are key, but they're also rear-view mirror metrics in many cases. If you have low retention rates, for example, that's a sign of a problem that's already happened (people have already left!) and all you can do is try to reverse course. To get ahead of such problems, many companies are using pulse surveys to gain more real-time insight. These are great tools, and in fact, despite all the digital age tools at our disposal, research shows that surveys are still one of the best ways to measure employee engagement.[8] We recommend them and use them ourselves, but with a caution about the importance of surveying with intention. That requires two key components: taking care that the survey itself is well designed (asking clear questions and knowing how you will use the answers), and ensuring you aren't surveying more often than you can actually act upon the results. If you survey too often, you run the risk of overtaxing your employees, giving them just one more item to add to their already long to-do lists, which can contribute to burnout. You also run the risk of undermining your intention: Pulse surveys are generally meant to communicate to people that you care about their feedback, but if employees repeatedly raise the same issues but don't see any progress being made, then they can have the opposite effect—they can end up being more demoralizing than productive.

A tactic that many companies have found useful is the "stay interview" rather than the "exit interview." We recommended something similar in Step 6, when suggesting that managers stage regular career growth conversations with each of their team members to better understand what motivates them and, crucially, whether they are feeling that motivation at this point in time. Another approach that we believe to be highly effective came to us from Tina Moore Gilbert, Managing Director at Management Leadership for Tomorrow (MLT). The company came up with three quick prompts designed to indicate how likely an employee is to stay at the company. So, instead of asking "how engaged are you" in a formal survey, try asking these simple true or false questions that can be answered in a matter of seconds:

- I feel like the organization invests in my development and advancement.
- I feel like I can succeed in my organization.
- I feel like I'm being positioned for long term career success.

In a flexible work world, leaders need to refocus on outcomes that will really drive engagement, and then, by extension, the success of the business. We have touched on a number of tools in these last steps that can be immediately applied to help you move from activity-based measures to outcomes, including: frequent check-ins; dashboards like BCG used and responsibility charts like the RACI matrix; pulse surveys and MLT's three-question prompt. These tools can all help you drive change in a transparent and engaging way. The objective here is to move the business forward while building a culture of trust and accountability. This means a fundamental change in the roles and responsibilities of managers, as well as a fundamentally different orientation for the company as a whole in order to make flexible work successful and unlock the potential of people throughout your organization.

Checklist for Step 7: Focus on the Outcomes

☑ Do you understand how old measurements based on activity and output can be getting in the way and undermining success in your company?

☑ Have you considered how you can balance measures of business outcomes—like revenue growth and profitability—with drivers of long-term performance—like employee engagement and customer satisfaction?

☑ Are you communicating to your managers about how to utilize outcome-based measures both for individuals and for their teams as a whole?

☑ Have you set up ways for measuring employee engagement on a regular basis?

Conclusion: Making a Difference

We believe that flexible work is the future, and there are a lot of reasons why businesses need to start embracing that future now. We have already talked through the top ones, including:

- Your people want it. Many of them need it. And increasingly they are going to expect it, or they will find it somewhere else.
- It's a competitive advantage that opens up your hiring pool far beyond commuting distance from the office. It makes it easier to attract, retain, and engage diverse, top talent.
- It helps unlock potential in more of your people, fostering inclusion and leveling the playing field, which leads to better outcomes.
- It's an opportunity to move to new ways of learning, connecting, collaborating, managing, and measuring that better supports your people and your business. Knowledge work has transformed businesses, but many business practices simply haven't kept up.
- A number of companies have already started down this path, and they are seeing higher employee engagement and better outcomes as a result.

But there's another reason, too, one that we have only touched on throughout this book, but that we think is worth considering before we send you on your way: Flexible work can make a real difference in people's lives, including your own. It has certainly made a difference in ours and many of the people we have encountered while focusing on this work.

That includes Erin Defay, Vice President of HR Tech at Dell Technologies. The company introduced a flexible, outcomes-based approach to working—which they call Connected Workplace—a decade before the pandemic. (In fact, when the pandemic hit, more than 64% of Dell employees already worked remotely one or more days a week.) The philosophy behind it is that "work is not a time or a place; it's the thing you do," according to Defay. That's a philosophy to which Defay says she owes her "career and growth." She's an active duty military spouse who has moved five times since she started with the company, to different cities, different time zones, even a different country for a while when her husband got posted to Japan. During the same period she had two children, and her flexible schedule made it possible for her to be available to them as well as to her work, which was especially important given the fact that her partner was deployed. Through it all she's been able to continue building her career because "Dell has been nothing but supportive." And she feels lucky given the sheer difficulty other military and so-called "trailing" spouses have in finding and keeping employment. For people in these kinds of situations, "having flexibility is life-changing," she says, and as a result "no company could lure me away."

For Anu Bharadwaj, Chief Operating Officer at Australia-originated software company, Atlassian, it was the opportunities for a different lifestyle that most appealed to her. Atlassian culture has always been very social and connected, so she missed her colleagues when Atlassian transitioned to remote work, but she also enjoyed the perks of being able to work from different places. "Having moved from Sydney to Mountain View in the Bay Area, I missed two things the most: my family and the beach," she explains, "so I worked from San Diego for a couple of months. Then I worked out of my sister's house in Minneapolis for a bit, and I really appreciated the extra hours I got to spend with my nephew after my work was done for the day. Our executive team was always distributed across countries, so my work was not disrupted in any way."

We've already told you the story of Mike Brevoort, who no longer felt like he had to travel dozens of times a year for executive meetings when Slack moved to Digital-First. And Harold Jackson, who was able to move back home to be with his family when flexible work policies finally—after years of trying—allowed him to.

It has made a difference in our lives, too. Flexible work gave Brian the opportunity to reset a balance that had been missing in his life for far too long. Over the course of more than two decades, he had made job decisions that were intended to get him more time with his family and take on more of the load of raising two kids, which often fell to his wife as the "default parent" in the relationship. But despite those good intentions, it wasn't until recently, after Slack embraced a Digital-First way of working, that it really "took."

For Sheela, the advice she received in business school—"to burn the candle at both ends at the expense of family and friends"—reinforced the career she didn't want to build. As a woman of color, work had always been broken for her, a place where she felt pressured to work twice as hard to make it half as far, to ignore comments made by others about whether she deserved her position, to hide the fact that, as a mother of two girls and a daughter of elderly parents, she had other responsibilities that pulled her in different directions. She was once on the brink of leaving the corporate world entirely, but now she feels like she can reclaim her power and build her work around her life, rather than the other way around.

For Helen, she never had a lot of role models early in her career to show her how to balance being a mother and being a person who wanted to continue to grow professionally—likely because there just weren't a lot of good options out there for doing so. Her first child was born just before the pandemic shut down offices, so she has luckily never needed to figure out how to be a new mom (with breastfeeding and regular baby doctor appointments) alongside navigating the old-fashioned 9-to-5, commute-to-the-office-everyday model. Instead, with both she and her husband working flexibly during the pandemic, they had a chance to build a more equal partnership in the family they were starting without having any one person feel like the "default parent" and making tradeoffs between childcare and career aspirations. Whereas they once wondered how they would handle even one child, they are now on their second and even contemplating number three!

These are just a few stories, but we've heard countless others with similar themes as we have become more and more focused on the benefits of flexible work. There is a deeply human desire in all of us to find out just what we're capable of and to really do our best work. It's a shame that so often old ideas about how work should be done get in the way of that. Because none of us are *just* workers after all. We're all human beings (with all the complexities that entails) who work. What we have all seen during this grand experiment that the pandemic forced upon us is that being given the power and the freedom to do our best work together can be transformative—for people *and* for the companies they work for.

Resources: Your Future of Work Toolkit

Following are the tools and templates referenced in this book. You can also go to **FutureForum.com/Book** to find these and additional resources online.

Step 1:   A Simple Framework for Creating Flexible Work Purpose and Principles

Step 2:   A Simple Framework for Creating Guardrails

          Do We Need a Meeting?

Step 3:   Team-Level Agreements Starter Template

Step 4:   Applying Design Thinking to Flexible Work Challenges

Step 5:   Creating Meetings that Matter

Step 6:   Tips to Inspire Trust, Create Clarity, and Unlock Potential on Your Team

          Personal Operating Manual

Step 7:   Measuring Outcomes

          Management Leadership for Tomorrow's 3-Question Prompt

          BCG's Team Success Survey

Step 1 Tool: A Simple Framework for Creating Your Flexible Work Purpose and Principles

While each company's principles will vary somewhat in sentiment and words in order to resonate with that company's culture and beliefs, we have found that they cover three main categories. Use this simple framework to ensure that your company's flexible work principles provide your people with the guidance they need to shift to a new way of working.

Type of principle	Why this is important	Starter prompts to ask your team	Company examples
Overarching intention of a shift in how we work	Used to re-articulate the importance of flexible work to the organization, and to set the groundwork for change	What is motivating this shift in how you work as a company? What words create a sense of urgency or groundswell for change?	**Royal Bank of Canada (RBC):** Flexible work is here to stay **Levi Strauss & Co.:** Flexibility is fundamental **Slack:** Embracing a Digital-First approach to work at Slack
How we are approaching this shift	Used to give leaders and employees a starting point for change, especially since flexible work upends so much of how we *used* to work and can be overwhelming to get started	What are mind-set shifts that leaders need to make? How does where you're going relate to current company values and priorities?	**RBC:** Starts with our business strategy **Levi Strauss & Co.:** The work drives the where **Slack:** ■ We aren't going back, we're moving forward with all that we've learned ■ Digital-First doesn't mean never in person ■ Progress, not perfection

Type of principle	Why this is important	Starter prompts to ask your team	Company examples
Main things we care about when considering what flexibility means to us	Used to highlight how we want flexibility to play out in the organization, and important flexibility considerations when making decisions at work, especially around people & opportunities	What results do you want to achieve with flexible work? What are important considerations or risks to highlight for people as they implement flexible work?	**RBC:** ■ Proximity still matters ■ Strategic investment is required ■ Inclusive culture with growth opportunities **Levi Strauss & Co.:** ■ Connection is key ■ Trust is the foundation ■ Lead with empathy and learn together **Slack:** ■ Flexibility: Provide flexibility & freedom for people to do their best work ■ Inclusivity: Ensure equitable access to opportunity and build inclusive teams ■ Connection: Slack is our headquarters

Step 2 Tool: A Simple Framework for Creating Guardrails

Type of guardrail	Why is this important	Starter prompts to ask your team	Example actions
Leadership guardrails	Flexible work is like just about anything else that's integral to your company's success: To make it work, leaders have to set the tone from the top. Without your leadership modeling the right behaviors, the principles you set will fail.	What are some behaviors that we, as leaders, need to model to further our principles? What are some behaviors we need to leave behind? What are some structural issues blocking us from modeling this behavior? How might we report back in with each other on adopting these guardrails?	Taking symbolic actions to further your principles Showing vulnerability and encouraging others to do the same Making a pledge and sticking with it
Workplace guardrails	In the world of flexible work, leaders need to redesign the role of the office. Setting guardrails keeps people from reverting back to old norms of work, and helps them see new potential for shared space.	What is the role of our shared space together? What do we want to keep? How do we design equitable meeting and collaboration experiences for distributed teams? What is the role of our offsites? How are we supporting leaders to foster connection during time together?	Aligning on the role of shared office space Investing in an equitable experience regardless of location Redesigning team offsites and meetings

Type of guardrail	Why is this important	Starter prompts to ask your team	Example actions
Culture guardrails	Creating a new flexible work strategy offers leaders the opportunity to address some challenges that have long been part of traditional workplace cultures. Now's the time to be intentional about the way in which you're crafting your culture.	What do our employees love most about our culture? What are some common trends for improvement? (e.g. burnout, meetings about meetings, internal decks) Where are we seeing greatest retention risks? Why? What do we want to keep and give away?	Evaluating the role of meetings Assessing how you foster creativity Studying promotion calibrations and what merits mobility Identifying common trends of perceived positive and negative behavior in last review cycle

Step 2 Tool: Do We Need a Meeting?

No one grew up dreaming of back-to-back, 9-to-5 meetings, whether virtual or in-person. Flexibility in when people work makes them more engaged and productive, and that requires developing new muscles around blending synchronous "bursts" of work together with individual "maker" time. The first step toward making space for focus time is to reduce the number of meetings we are collectively in. Always start with: "Do we really need to meet?"

Do we really need to meet? Some best practices:

- **Push status updates to in-channel** and instead use the /remind function or a Workflow to send regular prompts to the team for status updates.

- Similarly, **use a channel to share information** (presentations, documents, etc.) where you're speaking one to many, and instead consider using Stories or a recorded Zoom video to do voiceover for the content.

- Err on the side of **canceling recurring meetings**, or at minimum **ask to cancel if there is no agenda** prior to the meeting.

- Think about **what parts of a meeting can be done async beforehand** to make the time together more productive (e.g. pre-read, feedback in advance, come up with a set of ideas to bring to the discussion, etc.).

- **Be intentional about the meetings that do get created** to ensure you're making the most of the time you have together.

Framework for assessing meeting types

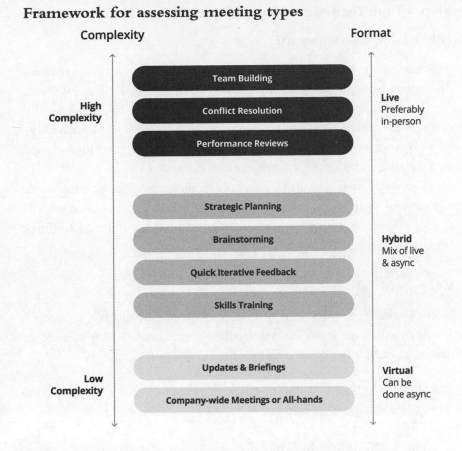

Figure Toolkit 1: "Do we need to meet" framework inspired by *Harvard Business Review*'s "When Do We Actually Need to Meet in Person?" (Rae Ringel, "When Do We Actually Need to Meet in Person?," *Harvard Business Review,* July 26, 2021.)

Step 3 Tool: Team-Level Agreements Starter Template

What Is This Document?

This template is for teams to create and document team-level agreements. Team-level agreements (sometimes called "Team Norms," "Team Working Agreements," or "Team Operating Manuals") are a set of guidelines that establish a working environment and allow teammates to understand how to work with one another. The goal of this document is to inspire trust, create clarity, and unlock performance on teams.

This template is designed to be flexible; please modify the template or add sections to meet your needs. Be mindful to share the document with all team members, and keep your agreements updated by soliciting feedback from new members who join your team.

Keep in Mind . . .

In our Digital-First world, the most successful teams are flexible, connected, and inclusive. Your team norms should accommodate a wide range of situations, including team members who:

Joined the company recently and . . .
- Hope to join office culture.
- Plan to work remotely.
- Plan to work from home some days and the office some days.
- Aren't sure yet what they want to do.

Were remote workers and . . .
- Hope to join office culture going forward.
- Plan to remain remote.
- Plan to work from home some days and the office some days.
- Aren't sure yet what they want to do.

Were office workers and . . .
- Hope to continue going forward.
- Plan to work remotely.
- Plan to work from home some days and the office some days
- Aren't sure yet what they want to do.

Team-Level Agreements Template
Values: What Do We Value in Our Working Environment as a Team?

As a team, we value working in an environment that . . .

- Allows everyone to participate fully whether in-person or remote
- Encourages continuous feedback
- Prioritizes and honors focus time

Tip: You may find that company values are a good starting point for the team values discussion, especially if your company has built and communicated a set of *principles and guardrails for flexible work* that point to more specific flexible work values.

Schedules & Meetings: How Will We Collaborate?

As a team, we have the following norms around our **schedules** . . .

- **Core collaboration hours:** We expect team members to be available for in-sync work between the hours of 10:00 a.m.–2:00 p.m. PT, Mondays through Thursdays
- **Dedicated focus time:** We prioritize and dedicate 2-hour focus time blocks from 1:00–3:00 p.m. PT, every weekday
- **Notifications:** We default to notifications off during non-core collaboration hours or focus time
- **Response time:** We set clear expectations for who needs to respond and when, and we reserve off-hours escalations for truly urgent issues, via text or phone call

Tip: Depending on your team, you may find that core collaboration hours are easier to define and manage versus trying to have a "no meetings Thursday" block, or vice versa! These agreements are not set in stone, and teams often find themselves experimenting and iterating with these initial arrangements as they settle into a working cadence.

As a team, we have the following norms around our **meetings and communication expectations . . .**

- One dials in, all dial in to a meeting to ensure that everyone is participating on an equal playing field
- We commit to creating agendas at least 24 hours in advance for all live (or synchronous) meetings
- Notes from meetings are always documented and shared back to the team
- More than two of us invited to another internal team's meeting? Others should feel free to decline

Tip: Meeting hygiene is a universal need, not just to make flexible work successful. Team's find that meeting and communications hygiene requires regular practice and pruning. "Meeting-creep" happens all too easily, and teams find it useful to dedicate time (e.g. monthly or quarterly) to review how they're doing and where they can be more proactive in decreasing meeting load (and related, zoom fatigue) while increasing dedicated focus time for deep work.

Accountability: How Do We Hold Each Other Accountable?

As a team, we want to set expectations and hold each other accountable in the following ways . . .

- We clearly define work and deliverable requirements from the beginning, including a primary owner (also known as a "DRI—directly responsible individual")
- We commit to making it clear when we need feedback (from whom and when)
- Every major project will have retrospective meetings to reflect on what went well, what could've been better, and what we've learned

> **Tip:** Flexible work is successful if teams are measuring success by outcomes, not by how many hours someone is working in a day. To do that, teams need to be focused on defining outcomes, roles, and responsibilities upfront and over-communicating as changes and different needs arise.

Relationships: Coming together as a team

As a team, we want to build our relationships with each other in the following ways . . .

- When it comes to bringing ourselves to work, we embrace vulnerability with boundaries. We operate from a place of trust—we can speak openly about our lives outside of work.
- We commit to celebrating one another's successes both publicly and within the team.
- We commit to being open and honest about when we are overloaded or need support, both personally and professionally.

> **Tip:** Focus on building team connection first within your immediate team, but consider expanding these agreements over time to find ways to intentionally connect with other teams across the organization (e.g. bringing in more regular guest speakers to team meetings, supporting more cross-team mentorship with senior leaders, and leveraging technology like Donut for adhoc coffee chat pairings).

Checking-in and evolving our team agreements over time

As a team, we want to check in on how things are going by . . .

- Spending part of our team meeting every month discussing our team-level agreements and getting feedback on what is and isn't working
- Creating a quarterly poll to get anonymous feedback across our department on our team-level agreements, and suggestions for improvement

Step 4 Tool: Applying Design Thinking to Flexible Work Challenges

Complex problems like creating flexibility for people, teams, and organizations require understanding the needs of the people involved, engaging them in generating ideas, and taking a hands-on approach to prototyping and testing those ideas.

There are six core stages, but it's also not a linear process, nor are you ever "done." This process requires a continuous-improvement approach.

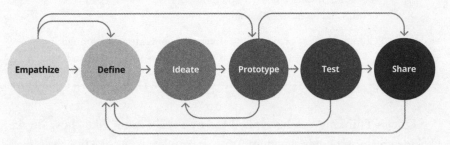

Stage	Definition	Examples of methodologies
Empathize	Develop an empathetic under-standing of the problem you are trying to solve.	Employee sentiment surveys, focus groups, and diary studies of people at work
		Listening sessions with diverse cross-sections of the organization
Define	Create a problem statement from your people's perspective	Analysis and synthesis of research, and identification of high impact challenges
		Test definitions of problem statements with the people you're trying to help
Ideate	Generate potential solutions	Start with "how might we solve . . ." questions
		Brainwriting (independent exercises gathered asynchronously) over brainstorming; "worst possible solution" exercises
		Internal as well as external benchmarks; what are high performance / high sentiment teams doing?

Stage	Definition	Examples of methodologies
Prototype	Build low cost, quick ways to build some of the solutions proposed	Enlist "pilot teams" of those willing to test new methodologies, tools, and processes
		Develop supporting infrastructure: workplace, IT, and HR needed to support tests, how to report out findings
Test	Execute on changes in small scale ways to not only measure results, but further refine options and problem definition	Run iterative tests in pilot teams, or side-by-side comparisons across teams
Share	Communicate the change	Internal communications through announcements, storytelling, and, as needed, policy or infrastructure changes

Design Thinking can be applied to large-scale issues, like "how do we provide greater schedule flexibility," or to narrower issues, like the challenges faced by people attending so-called "hybrid meetings" (meetings where some of the team is in an office and others are dialing in).

Here's an example:

Stage	Definition
Empathize	Employees dialing-in to meetings with in-office participants find it hard to track what's being discussed in the room, hard to "break in," and fear being left out.

Employees in the office find they lack access to the documents shared in the video tool, and miss access to chat. |
| Define | Employees need a level playing field for participation in hybrid meetings. |
| Ideate | Wide range of potential solutions created; a few examples:
■ All meetings are held in-office or all-remote, no "hybrid" allowed.
■ iPads on stands in conference rooms for each employee who dials in.
■ Upgrade all conference rooms with large scale immersive systems
■ "One Dials In, All Dial In" guidelines combined with best practices for teams. |

Stage	Definition
Prototype	Found two teams to test a variety of different low-cost configurations of hybrid meeting setups with some participants in conference rooms, some remote. ■ All on laptops, all mics open ■ All on laptops, in-room usage of microphone & screen ■ All on laptops, in-room usage of microphone only ■ Room on A/V system, external people dialed in
Test	Ran through variants of prototype tests, which created not only feedback but new problems (neck strain in conference rooms) and new solutions (laptop stands).
Share	All of the work above was done in a public Slack channel (#pilot-digital-first), and when the prototypes settled into a best practice, shared through announcements internally, shared publicly on social media and established a physical reminder by installing laptop stands in conference rooms.

Step 5 Tool: Creating Meetings that Matter

Adapted from advice provided by facilitator, strategic advisor, and podcast host, Parker, who is the author of *The Art of Gathering: How We Meet and Why it Matters*.[1]

First, ask yourself: Do we really need a meeting?

Refer back to the tool for Step 2 to ensure, first and foremost, that a meeting is necessary and that you're not just taking up time in people's schedules.

Second, start with the basics: What is the purpose of the meeting? Who needs to be there? And who decides?

"The biggest mistake we make when we gather is we assume the purpose of the gathering is shared and obvious," says Parker. It's common to skip over basic questions like:

- What is the purpose of meeting?
- Who needs to be there?
- Who gets to decide?

These may seem like simple questions, but Parker contends they're complex—even profound. Asking them presents teams with an opportunity for positive growth and change.

Parker recommends holding listening sessions with your team to facilitate open discussions around prompts like:

- During the last 20 months of disruption and change, what did we miss most about not being able to be in the office?
- What did we not miss—what are we ready to discard?
- What did we invent during the pandemic that we want to carry forward?
- What new practices do we want to create now?

"Debate it. Discern it," says Parker. "And then run a series of experiments."

Third, every gathering is a social contract. Your role as host is to help participants understand what is expected of them.

"Yes, gathering is about connection, but it's also about power," says Parker. "Pretending power dynamics don't exist will make you a less artful gatherer." As a leader, it's on you to deliberately design an environment that levels power inequities and invites people to contribute by doing the following:

- Understand ahead of time the different contexts people bring. "If I'm at home and my child is napping in another room and my colleagues are in the office chit-chatting and drinking coffee together before the meeting starts, that is an unequal power dynamic."

- Acknowledge the challenges. For example: "Hybrid gatherings aren't one gathering—they're three," she says. "There's the experience of the people in the room together. There's the virtual experience. And then there's the mix of those people interacting. You need to acknowledge that people are living in different realities."

- Assign a meeting facilitator, and, for larger, hybrid gatherings, up to three distinct facilitators—a host to facilitate on the ground, a second host to consider the needs of virtual attendees, and a third dedicated to fostering the mix between the two.

- Make the rules clear and public. Being explicit about the rules—such as when and how to ask questions, when is casual conversation encouraged, when to keep your video on, and when it's ok to turn it off—overrides unspoken cultural norms, gives everyone clarity on what is expected, and leads to greater psychological safety.

Fourth, for transformation to occur, you must have some element of risk. "I'm most interested in transformative gatherings, when people come in one way and leave slightly altered by their experience," says Parker. But true transformation requires some healthy controversy. "Unhealthy peace is as damaging as unhealthy conflict," Parker contends.

To encourage teams to display what she calls "generous heat" or "generous controversy," Parker recommends asking the following questions, devised by experience designer, Ida Benedetto. Before a team gathering, ask yourself:

- What is this group avoiding?
- What is the gift in helping them face it?
- Is the gift worth the risk?
- Can I help the team confront this with care?

Step 6 Tool: Tips to Inspire Trust, Create Clarity, and Unlock Potential on Your Team

Most managers are not trained to lead distributed teams and need hands–on training to shift from gatekeeper to coach. The three core tenants of the "Manager as Coach" are:

Ultimately, you know your team best, so we expect you to leverage your knowledge of your team dynamics and individual working styles to support your employees in the way that makes most sense for you. Below are a few tips for inspiring trust, creating clarity, and unlocking potential on your team.

Inspire Trust: Build a Culture of Psychological Safety

Tips to Try Today to Model and Encourage Vulnerability

With Your Team:

- **Create drop-in sessions:** Create office hours or "drop-in" sessions for your reports where they can connect outside of regular meetings. You can use the appointment feature in the calendar if you want to give folks privacy or just create a meeting that people can opt-in to attend.

- **Set up reminders to check in with your team:** You might realize by the end of the week that you haven't spoken to one of your direct reports. Even if it's just a quick "hello, how are you?" make sure to check-in with each direct report.

- **Check in periodically:** Here are a few recurring questions you can ask in your 1:1s: *How are you doing this week? Has anything changed about your situation that you want to share? How can I be supporting you better? What's working for you? What isn't working?*

As a Leader:

- **Share what's hard:** In your team meeting, tell your team what's been challenging for you, what keeps you up at night, what your work day looks like. There's no need to overshare with your team, but merely articulating what you're working through can be really helpful in making your team feel connected to you and safe to share their own authentic experiences and feelings.

- **Ask for help (so others will too!):** Asking for help is one of the easiest ways to demonstrate vulnerability. Come to your next team meeting with a question or problem that your team can help solve. A few examples: *How can we make our meetings more productive? More inclusive? Do we want to modify how we check-in on progress as a team? If so, how? Where do we think there are silos of information and how can I help break those down? Do you feel like you're missing context on any of your projects? How can I help you get that context? How can I be a better leader to you all?*

- **Create spaces for human connection:** Sharing your human experience requires a high degree of vulnerability. The more we learn about each other as humans, the more connected we feel and the more trust we build. Many of these techniques can be seen under the "Remove feelings of isolation" section (icebreaker activities, Zoom happy hours, etc.) but you can also weave these moments of human connection into your meetings and check-ins.

Create Clarity: Make Feedback the Norm

Tips to Try Today to Normalize Feedback

- **Schedule weekly feedback meetings with your reports:** This might feel like overkill at first, but even taking the first 5–10 minutes of your weekly 1:1s to provide feedback can help your team members stay on track and be productive and building this habit makes it easier over time. You can always solicit feedback by asking: What can I do to be a better manager to you and the team? And you can always give feedback on: Here's one thing you can focus on this week.

- **Model healthy conflict:** Remote work can make employees even more conflict-avoidant but harmony doesn't force us to think outside the box or innovate. Researchers argue that avoiding confrontation leads to "conflict debt" that stalls productivity. If a disagreement comes up in a meeting, don't shy away from it by "taking it offline" or discussing it later. Let people respectfully share their opinions giving both parties the space and opportunity to share their sides and moderate the conversation by remaining calm and acknowledging both perspectives.

- **Leverage "IRL" conversations.** If a thread or discussion is getting out of hand (things are becoming increasingly unclear, emotions are escalating, the right people aren't looped into the conversation), call a "time out" on the conversation and move it to a call or videoconference. Or bring up the topic at your next in-person offsite.

- **Schedule Stay Interviews.** Schedule longer 1:1s with team members who are at higher risk of attrition, with an emphasis on discovery and inquiry. Pose direct questions to gather feedback on what's working and what's not: *What do you like about your job? What gives you energy? What saps your energy? If you could change something about your job, what would it be? What would make your job more satisfying? What opportunities will help you stretch and grow? How might I, as your manager, help you get there?*

Unlock Potential: Build Equitable Policies and Practices

Tips to Try Today to Set Boundaries

- **Create a meeting policy document to keep focus:** Sometimes the temptation to respond quickly to something creeps up during meetings. Make it clear that multitasking on calls isn't OK. Digital-First communication, like in-person communication, requires everyone on a call to be mentally present and engaged. Write down your rules in your Team Level Agreement.

- **Experiment with timing:** Meeting lengths tend to be arbitrarily chosen in increments of 30 minutes and we tend to expand our meetings to fill up the time allotted. Try reducing one hour meetings by 10 minutes, or stick to a strict agenda and end the meeting when agenda items are complete.

- **Post your schedule:** Be open and honest about what your new schedule looks like and your availability throughout the day. Your reports will appreciate the transparency and be more thoughtful about their own schedules.

- **Turn the video off:** Sometimes a simple phone call can do the trick and fight the video fatigue. Encourage your teammates to take walking phone calls as a way to break up the day.

Step 6 Tool: Personal Operating Manual (POM) Worksheet

What Is It?

Operating/User Manuals are short, professional documents that aim to help teams learn how to work better together by offering explicit descriptions of personal values and communication styles.

POMs are most effective when they are short, succinct, and scannable. Ideally, they should fit on a single page and the text should be active and engaging.

Why Do It?

A POM can help teams:

- Build psychological safety
- Improve communication
- Provide insight into individual motivations
- Enable better collaboration
- Foster empathy
- Avoid misunderstandings

A POM can also shorten the learning curve for new employees joining a team. A POM is not a replacement for face-to-face connection. Before you share your POM make sure you have a conversation with the person you're sharing it with. That discussion is meant to inform the context and purpose of the document as well as listen to reactions from team members.

How to Make One?

A POM consists of bullets and short descriptions that describe the following six things:

- My work style
- What I value
- How to best communicate with me
- What people misunderstand about me
- What I don't have patience for
- How to help me

Read through the following reference questions for more details on each category and to get inspiration. Though you can go ahead and just start writing your POM, it's best if you spend a few minutes reflecting on how you like to work, how you communicate, and what things you value.

POM: Brainstorm

Before creating your user manual, spend a few minutes working through the steps below to identify some of the words, concepts, and values that define you.

Step 1: How to best describe me (my work style, what people misunderstand about me)

Circle or highlight all the phrases which apply to you.

Cautious	Relaxed	Persuasive
Deliberate	Personable	Expressive
Analytical	Competitive	Detailed
Formal	Tenacious	Direct
Curious	Diligent	Inventive
Inquisitive	Disciplined	Friendly
Precise	Purposeful	Flexible
Introverted	Systematic	Supportive
Extroverted	Driven	Focused
Compassionate	Resilient	Organized
Empathetic	Sociable	Creative
Encouraging	Passionate	Resourceful
Collaborative	Attuned	Intuitive
Patient	Enthusiastic	Logical
Courageous	Hospitable	Adaptable
Direct	Impatient	Argumentative

What other characteristics would describe/not describe you:

Step 2: My catchphrase (how to best communicate with me, how to help me)

Circle or highlight all the phrases which apply to you.

Be well prepared	Give me time to respond	Be genuine
Put things in writing	Give me the high level overview	Be proactive
Give me the details		Speak clearly
Be direct & concise	Be patient	Take time to listen
Focus on the results	Get to know me first	Be transparent
Always be honest	Solicit & listen to my opinions	Solicit input from others
Don't exaggerate		
Be patient & supportive	Be mindful of my time	Ask questions
	Challenge my opinions	Embrace different opinions
Ask for my input	Talk to me privately	
Be friendly	Talk to me in public	Celebrate wins
Be engaging	Give me feedback	Provide solutions
Be open-minded	Allow me to give feedback	Suggest efficiencies
		Share your innovations
	Keep it positive	I take too long to act or respond.

What other phrases would describe/not describe my catchphrase:

Step 3: My Values (what I value, what I don't have patience for)

Circle or highlight all the phrases which apply to you.

Resiliency	Diversity	Coaching others
Curiosity	Honesty	Motivating others
Collaboration	Clarity	Protecting others
Grit	Creativity	Advocating for others
Positivity	Hospitality	Being acknowledged
Directness	Discipline	Being understood
Courage	Health	Being diplomatic
Compassion	Drive	Being vulnerable
Innovation	Adaptability	Seeing others learn
Resourcefulness	Kindness	Seeing others succeed
Inclusion	Growth mindset	Seeing others happy
Authenticity	Diverse opinions	Talking over others
Transparency	Having equality	Avoiding conflict
Humor	Self-Serving	Passive-Aggressiveness
Safety	Ambition	Being condescending

What other words or phrases would describe/not describe my values:

POM: Prompts—Reference Questions and Details

These prompts can give inspiration to help fill out your POM. You don't need to answer all the questions. Instead, look through the lists and see if any are particularly relevant to you and use them in formulating your responses.

My work style

- How would people who work with you describe your presence in the office?

- Are you introverted or outgoing at work, or something else entirely?

- What style of working gives you the most energy, or harnesses your passions?

- Are you led by logic or emotion; data or intuition?

- Do you gravitate toward thinking about the big picture or the small details?

- How does work fit into the rest of your life; is there a strong work-life divide for you, or do they run together?

- Of personality or "type-based" tests you've taken in the past, what do their results reveal about your approach to work?

- If someone you know outside of work asked you, "What are you like at the office?," what would you tell them?

What I value

- What are some of the qualities of people you admire or strive to be like? (Those qualities are likely your values.)

- Think of your favorite person to work with—what qualities make them this way?

- What attributes do you seek in a team or in a manager?

- Are there any "deal breakers" that would cause you to leave a job? Knowing those may lead you to understand what you care deeply about.

- What actions display the opposite/flip-side of your values?

What I don't have patience for

- Think of the last time something or someone drove you crazy. What about the situation or person led you to feel that way?

- When you feel annoyed at work, what kinds of things have led you there?

- What else do you find hard to tolerate in people who you work with?

How to best communicate with me

- What levels of directness or tact do you strive for in your own communication? And what levels do you seek in others?

- Think of the best experience you had where someone gave you feedback. What did they do that worked well for you?

- What do people need to do to "really get through to you" with a message?

- Think of someone whose communication style drives you crazy. Use that to identify what you do seek in good communication.

What people misunderstand about me

- When people get a first impression of you, what do they frequently get wrong?

- What does your team probably not know about your inner workings that you wish they understood?

- When you think of how people would describe you at work, what's missing from their list?

How to help me

- Think of a time when something got really hard for you at work. What could others have done to make that easier for you?

- What is a weakness you have, and how might others help you manage that?

- What are you insecure about at work? What things can your team do so that insecurity doesn't hold you back?

POM Template

POMs are short, professional documents that aim to help teams learn how to work better together by offering an explicit description of one's personal values and communication styles.

My work style

- Statement 1
- Statement 2
- Statement 3

What I value

- Statement 1
- Statement 2
- Statement 3

How to best communicate with me

- Statement 1
- Statement 2
- Statement 3

How to help me

- Statement 1
- Statement 2
- Statement 3

What I don't have patience for

- Statement 1
- Statement 2
- Statement 3

What people misunderstand about me

- Statement 1
- Statement 2
- Statement 3

Step 7 Tool: Measuring Outcomes

We need to help managers move away from measuring performance based on inputs (hours logged, presenteeism) and outputs (tickets closed, calls made) and instead to outcomes that impact your customers, employees, and business goals. What follows are some examples of methods companies are using to help managers move to an outcomes-driven way of ensuring success in a world of flexible work.

Individual Level

- **Onboarding:** Set clear goals for the first 30, 60 and 90 days. Goals should include learning about the company, function, and team through establishing relationships, access to historical knowledge, and groups to join. Starting goals and interim milestones should establish a clear, mutual understanding of objectives and methods.

- **Clear roles and responsibilities:** Ensure individuals understand their roles relative to their functional teams and in cross-functional assignments. Leverage RACI matrices to ensure clarity about whether the employee is Responsible, Accountable, Consulted, or Informed on key projects.

- **Goals and priorities:** Leverage weekly one-on-ones to check progress against goals and ensure alignment on priorities. Share progress updates across the team, including clear statements of prioritization to avoid confusion or identify potential conflicts for management resolution.

Team Level Performance and Team Dynamics

- **Team-level goals:** Teams, like individuals, need clear goals. Ensure alignment by publishing both longer-term goals (ex., quarterly) and interim goals or milestones (ex., biweekly). Publish key metrics—the three to five most important metrics used to measure progress—publicly, not only to the team, but to cross-functional stakeholders. Examples might include sales targets, product adoption, and recruiting pipeline.

- **Priorities:** Establish clear priorities across the goals and across key projects. Share status on key projects in public forums. Encourage escalations and turn the weekly "status check" into an escalation-resolution meeting. Track performance against goals set for top 10 projects.

- **Team health metrics:** Establish regular habits for team-level improvement of processes and group dynamics, for example "blockers" reviews in weekly check-ins: resource conflicts, business issues, or decisions that need to be made to enable progress. Run "blameless retrospectives"—postmortem assessments that focus on what was done well and opportunities for improvement, but not on who to blame for hiccups—for all major projects (eg., the big quarterly release) and share the results publicly.

Employee Engagement

- **Recruiting:** Measure key elements of your ability to target and hire talent. Metrics should include factors like quality applicant growth, offer yield, time to hire, and growth in the diversity of offers and acceptances.

- **Employee retention:** Track performance on unwanted attrition, overall attrition, and where employees move to next to understand potential drivers and competitive dynamics. Establish exit interviews and understand how drivers change over time. Make sure to look deeply at attrition in diverse populations both for trends and causes.

- **Employee engagement:** While overall job satisfaction can be a misleading metric, it's still important to measure and track against key internal and external changes (eg., policy shifts, business performance, competitive dynamics). Better yet, make use of Net Promoter Scores among your teams: Are employees willing to recommend working here to friends? Perhaps most tellingly, are they excited about the future of your company?

- **Understand key drivers of job satisfaction**: Measure employee attitudes around key issues: Can I do great work here? Do I have access to the information and people I need to be effective? Do I believe that the organization invests in my development? Can I succeed here? Am I being positioned for long-term career success?

Business Outcomes

- **Key financial metrics:** Look at key areas like: How has revenue growth changed? Which sectors are seeing the highest results—and why? Understand and share goals for margins and profitability, and clearly articulate tradeoffs between growth and bottom line results.

- **Performance against Environmental, Societal and Governance (ESG) and Diversity, Equity and Inclusion (DE&I) goals:** How are you articulating your ESG goals and tracking performance against them, internally as well as externally? Are you setting clear DE&I goals, and who is responsible for their performance? What benchmarking tools are you using? Which elements of ESG and DE&I are most important to you and how will you share progress internally and externally?

- **Customer success:** As you make changes to ensure employees are more engaged, continue to look at and compare with what's happening to customer satisfaction, net customer retention, and growth rates of your business.

- **Roadmap:** As you make changes to a more flexible workplace, establish metrics and ways to track progress against historical norms for your product roadmap, your sales pipeline, and your employee experience. Which areas are thriving in a new way of working, and which teams are struggling? How will that impact your overall goals as a business?

Step 7 Tool: Management Leadership for Tomorrow's 3-Question Prompt

While the employee engagement section above shows how you can measure employee reaction to new, flexible policies, those metrics are only a rear-view mirror. Designed by Management Leadership for Tomorrow to get a quick read on how likely an employee is to stay at your company, these quick-and-easy questions can be answered *true* or *false*:

- I feel like the organization invests in my development and advancement.
- I feel like I can succeed in my organization.
- I feel like I'm being positioned for long term career success.

Step 7 Tool: BCG's Team Success Survey

BCG project teams do either a weekly or biweekly survey of each team on key success metrics. The success metrics have to do with company culture as well as with the individual's sense of accomplishment and value to the organization, their ability to learn and develop, and the degree of psychological safety they feel with their managers and team members: Each person is asked to respond on a 1 to 4 scale where 1 = agree, 2 = tend to agree, 3 = tend to disagree, and 4 = disagree.

- I am having an overall positive experience on this project.
- In this team, we focus on outcomes and deliver client value.
- I am satisfied with my personal growth and learning.
- My skillset and contributions are valued by the team.
- In this team, I feel we behave with integrity and make decisions in line with BCG values.
- I feel comfortable speaking up in the team.
- I am doing the things I need to enable myself to thrive.
- My team exhibits care for each other.
- My team provides a supportive and inclusive environment.
- My team works together efficiently and effectively.

- My team has a clear, common understanding of our roles, priorities, and goals.

- The workload was sustainable for me this past week(s).

- I feel I have predictability in the way I work that allows me to stick to personal plans and key performance indicators.

- The senior executive responsible for the work and the full partnership team are engaged in ensuring a positive experience.

- My team regularly reviews our working model and travel cadence to ensure that it is intentional, provides value to our client, and encourages our team's collaboration.

- I can have open discussions with my team about travel and colocation plans, which make me feel supported.

Acknowledgments

When the three of us banded together to start Future Forum, we weren't sure where the adventure would take us. Little did we know that we would be joined by so many people who believe in redesigning work and the opportunities it brings, and have been willing to roll up their sleeves with us, openly share their experiences, and tell us what they've learned. Without their stories, this book would have never come to life.

In addition to the decades of experience and research conducted on the topic, the book is a product of the work of the Future Forum team, from the playbooks and reports to the working groups. We are grateful to everyone on our team who joined us in building Future Forum and put their own sweat and tears into the work, especially Dave Macnee, Maddy Cimino, Eliza Sarasohn, Taryn Brymn, Jack Hansley, Katarina Stucker, and Ali Aills.

Our insights are rooted in work driven by the world's greatest research team, led by Christina Janzer, Lucas Puente, and Mark Rivera. Beyond the research itself and a summary of findings, they've brought their own storytelling skills to the work. They've also been instrumental in helping us build relationships with academic experts, many of whom are quoted throughout this book.

Without the sponsorship, encouragement, and prodding of our "Board," this book, and our work overall, would not exist. We owe a tremendous amount of gratitude to Stewart Butterfield and David Schellhase, who got us off the ground, shared ideas as well as feedback, and ensured that we've "never been better." They were joined by Robby Kwok, Jonathan Prince, Nadia Rawlinson, Julie Liegl, Bob Frati, and Tamar Yehoshua, who have been instrumental partners along the way.

Future Forum isn't just the work of a bunch of Slack people and their passion to make work simpler, more pleasant, and more productive. We've been joined by partners who believe we have the opportunity of a lifetime to make work better for people. Thanks to the team at Boston Consulting Group led by Debbie Lovich, MillerKnoll led by Ryan Anderson and Joseph White, and Management Leadership for Tomorrow led by Tina Gilbert and Kevin Donahue. They've contributed their own expertise, findings, and energy to amplify our combined message.

A book written by three co-authors is an act of collaboration that requires a challenging blend of clarity of roles combined with willingness to mix it up and share blunt feedback. It wouldn't have worked if we didn't know each other as individuals, but more importantly it never would have come together without the hard work, prodding, and expertise that Christa Bourg brought to the work. Christa persevered through neophyte authors, an overabundance of input, and our tendency to write 500 words when 50 would suffice.

We found Christa, and got our bearings in being authors, through the guidance and support of our amazing agent Katherine Flynn. Without Katherine's involvement in the early stages, we wouldn't have gotten off the ground. And without Adam Grant's support, we'd never have found Katherine in the first place. Beyond adoring his work, we also know Adam is the world's most proficient and supportive networker.

Writing a book had been bouncing around in our heads since we started Future Forum. But it took a spark to light the fire, and Mike Campbell at Wiley provided that spark. We have managed to annoy Mike on multiple occasions with wanting to blow up how publishing works, and have jointly discovered what every author quickly figures out—writing a book is hard, titles and cover art are impossible. The visuals in the book are also essential ingredients for telling the story, and we have Alec Babala to thank for his art, and his patience as we changed our minds more than a few times. We're also grateful to Dawn Kilgore, our fantastic managing editor at Wiley.

Books that rely on research are grounded in fact. But the storytelling we've been able to do here is what we hope brings the ideas from that research to life. We're eternally grateful to those who were willing to open up their own stories, especially Mike Brevoort, Stewart Butterfield, Cal Henderson, Harold Jackson, and Dawn Sharifan at Slack. We share what we've learned along the way through how-to playbooks—dozens of them.

Those are built on the foundations laid by our amazing coworkers at Slack, including Ted Getten, Ariel Hunsberger, Jade Hanley, Ross Harmes, Evelyn Lee, Dawn Sharifan, Kristen Swanson, Sar Warner, and many more. No one would ever see that work if we hadn't been blessed with the partnership of Audrey Carson, Jessica Lehrman, Julie Mullins, Steve Sharpe, and Cyndi Wheeler.

Some of the most fun we had on the entire journey was one "meeting" with Amanda Atkins, Anna Pickard, and Jared Schwartz. Yes, we loved the title you came up with together. No, we didn't use it. We'll do better next time. Anna also pointed out that the original Future Forum manifesto was the kind of thing we shouldn't write—overly corporate jargon-dependent—so we've eliminated it from this book, and from all of existence. Thank you for reminding us of the importance of sounding human.

Getting executives to talk on the record about their challenges is not an easy task, but so many of them wanted to share so that others could learn. We hope we've done justice to their stories; they're all forces for good in the world: Rachael Allison and Angela Palermo of Genentech, Anu Bharadwaj at Atlassian, Melanie Collins and Alastair Simpson at Dropbox, Erin Defay at Dell, Helena Gottschling at Royal Bank of Canada, Nickle LaMoreaux of IBM, Tracy Layney at Levi Strauss & Co., and Mariano Suarrez-Battan at MURAL.

Very few of the ideas in this book originated with us. Besides the habits and practices of the companies we've worked with, the research in this book stands on the shoulders of experts. A big thanks to Raj Choudhury, Heidi Gardner, Adam Grant, Pamela Hinds, Brian Lowery, Priya Parker, Leslie Perlow, Ella Washington, and Anita Woolley.

There's also three of us, who each brought our own passion and perspective to the work, supported by many others.

Brian:

The right place to start is at the beginning. My parents had me when they were kids themselves, and I've been eternally grateful for their love and support. My mom, Becky Bryan, is my hero. She ended up raising two kids on her own, going back to school and holding down jobs, getting advanced degrees and leading organizations that supported cancer patients and eventually a hospice—emotionally challenging work. I remember some great summer talks with my dad, Bill Elliott, about teams at work and how to build them, lessons that stuck to today. My brother Matt was the tag-along who became a great friend, and an awesome husband and father.

I'm eternally grateful to Helen and Sheela for joining me on this journey. I couldn't have asked for two better cofounders. I've learned so much from each of you, personally and professionally. Writing a book while working full time is challenging; doing that while also raising young kids and having another kid is nearly impossible. You bring your own passion to the work, but also depth of expertise and openness to learn. I could not ask for better partners.

My own kids, Connor and Riley, aren't really kids anymore; they are amazing young men whose company I cherish, even if I don't get half of their jokes anymore.

All too often, I've lived to work instead of working to live. I worry about the signal that's sent to my children, and I hope what I've learned over the past few years will help bring back a sense of balance for them. And no one's paid more of a price for that than my partner, spouse, and best friend Maureen. Because work commitments felt inflexible, too often I wasn't there, truly there, in ways that were meaningful. Some of that changed over the years, as I learned what "default parent" meant (and that I wasn't one). Writing this book, and building Future Forum, is part of my continuing path of learning and growth. No one's been more instrumental on that path than Maureen. Thank you for being my coach, supporter, and the love of my life.

Sheela:

For my parents, Ramamoorthy and Shyamala, work was not meant to be a source of fulfillment. As immigrants to this country, it was what they had to do to provide for their families, but they left their jobs at the door when they walked into our home every evening. Their work ethic was one that my brother and I strived to emulate, but it was the prioritization of family, friends, and community that stuck with us the most. I thank them for providing me the opportunity to define the role of work in my life on my own terms, something they were never able to do. And I thank my brother, Satish, for encouraging me to never quit during the most challenging of moments.

And Brian and Helen: Remember when we embarked on this Future Forum journey and had no idea where it would take us? I'd say that this path has exceeded all of our expectations. Your friendship means the world to me and has been a highlight of my career. Thank you.

To my husband, partner, and best friend, Eric—thank you for embodying what true partnership looks like. Aside from being a constant source of encouraging Eric-isms that border on Ted Lasso cheesiness, you've never made me feel like professional ambition and hands-on parenting are mutually exclusive. Kudos for (incessantly) reminding me of the best legacy I can leave our girls and nieces: showing them that women don't have to "play the game"—we have the power to change the nature of "the game" itself.

And to my magical daughters, nieces, and all of the women in my life who will do amazing things—you are the source of inspiration for this book. I am cheering you on.

Helen:

I would not be here, in a position to shape a better way to work for myself and the people around me, if not for my parents Edward and Ann Lee. Dad, you flew 300 miles each way between LA and SF each week to get to work. Mom, you held two jobs for most of my childhood between the retail shop in Chinatown and the graveyard shift at the post office. I still don't know how you balanced all of that while creating a loving and supportive home for my brother and me to grow and learn in. Thank you a million times over.

Sheela and Brian, I still pinch myself wondering if all of this is real. Writing a book, creating a movement—these are amazing opportunities. But getting to do all of this with two people whom I deeply admire (and look up to, everyday!) has been such a privilege. Thank you for inspiring me every day with how you show up as leaders, friends, and people.

Thank you, Nate—my husband, partner, best friend, and loudest cheerleader. Even though I always say "no more pep talks," thank you for always believing in me and pushing me. You've never let me sacrifice my own ambitions to "just be a mom," and you've spent countless hours "getting coffee with Ethan" or "gardening with Ethan" to carve out space for me to think, to write, to work, and to sometimes just work out. Thank you for doing your best to take on the mental load and show me, through everyday actions, what equal partnership feels like.

To my son and baby girl, you are my reason. I want to be the mom who shows up equally at home and work. I want to carve a path for both of you to define work-life on your own terms. And I want to be here to soak up every moment—big and small—of our lives together.

Cast of Experts

Executives

Rachael Allison, People Strategy Lead, Genentech

Ryan Anderson, VP Global Research & Insights, MillerKnoll Inc.

Anu Bharadwaj, Chief Operating Officer, Atlassian

Stewart Butterfield, CEO and co-founder of Slack

Melanie Collins, Chief People Officer, Dropbox

Erin Defay, Vice President of HR Tech, Dell Technologies

Tina Gilbert, Managing Director, Management Leadership for Tomorrow

Helena Gottschling, Chief Human Resources Officer, Royal Bank of Canada (RBC)

Cal Henderson, Chief Technology Officer and co-founder of Slack

Nickle LaMoreaux, Chief Human Resource Officer, IBM

Tracy Layney, Chief Human Resources Officer, Levi Strauss & Co.

Debbie Lovich, Managing Director and Senior Partner, Boston Consulting Group

Darren Murph, Head of Remote, Gitlab

Dominic Price, Work Futurist, Atlassian

Dawn Sharifan, Head of People, Slack

Alastair Simpson, Vice President of Design, Dropbox

Mariano Suarez-Battan, Co-founder and CEO of MURAL

Joseph White, Director of Design Strategy, MillerKnoll Inc.

Academics and Thought Leaders

Prithwiraj Choudhury, Associate Professor at Harvard Business School and author of "Our Work-from-Anywhere Future"

Amy Edmondson, Professor of Leadership and Management at Harvard Business School and author of *The Fearless Organization: Creating Psychological Safety in the Workplace for Learning, Innovation, and Growth*

Heidi Gardner, Distinguished Fellow at Harvard Law School and author of *Smarter Collaboration* (Harvard Business Review Press, 2022)

Adam Grant, Professor at The Wharton School, author of *Think Again: The Power of Knowing What We Don't Know*, and host of the "WorkLife" podcast

Brian Lowery, Senior Associate Dean of Stanford University Graduate School of Business and host of the "Know What You See" podcast

Tsedal Neeley, Professor at Harvard Business School and author of *Remote Work Revolution: Succeeding from Anywhere*

Priya Parker, Founder at Thrive Labs and author of *The Art of Gathering: How We Meet and Why It Matters*

Leslie Perlow, Professor at Harvard Business School and author of *Sleeping with Your Smartphone: How to Break the 24/7 Habit and Change the Way You Work*

Ella Washington, Professor at Georgetown University McDonough School of Business and CEO of Ellavate Solutions

Anita Williams Woolley, Associate Professor of Organizational Behavior and Theory at Carnegie Mellon Tepper School of Business and author of *Collective Intelligence*

About the Authors

Brian Elliott

Brian Elliott is the Executive Leader and Senior Vice President of Future Forum, a consortium launched by Slack to help companies reimagine work in the new Digital-First world. Previously, Brian was the VP & General Manager of Platform at Slack, where he oversaw Platform strategy and execution. The Slack Platform integrates with enterprise tools from companies such as Google, Microsoft, Oracle, Salesforce, and Workday, as well as more than 2,300 other tools and services.

Before Slack, Brian was General Manager of Google Express, Google's full stack commerce platform, driving product, engineering, operations, and go-to-market functions. Prior to Google, Brian was CEO at startups like Monsoon Commerce, a software platform that services thousands of online businesses, and Alibris, a global ecommerce marketplace. Before that, Brian was a consultant with Boston Consulting Group.

Brian received a BA in Mathematics and Economics from Northwestern University and an MBA from Harvard Business School. His work has been published and cited in *Harvard Business Review*, *Fortune*, the *Economist,* and the *New York Times*. Brian and his partner Maureen are the proud parents of two fantastic young men and Yuki, the wonder dog.

Sheela Subramanian

Sheela Subramanian is a Vice President of Future Forum. Prior to this role, Sheela spent five years at Slack in several leadership roles, including as the Head of Global Enterprise Marketing, where she led the company's shift to a B2B organization. She also led the Product Marketing team, launching Slack in the enterprise segment and in dozens of new countries.

Before Slack, Sheela led growth and operations at several global startups focused on connectivity in emerging markets. She started her career at Google, where she drove marketing and strategy for a range of products. Most notably, she co-founded the Global Market Development team, where she led global and multicultural go-to-market efforts for the company.

Sheela received a BA from Stanford University and an MBA from Harvard Business School. She is a vocal advocate of workplace equity and serves on the Board of Stanford's Center for Studies in Race and Ethnicity. Her work is published and cited in *Fast Company*, the *Wall Street Journal*, the *New York Times*, and *Inc*. She is the proud mom of two magical daughters and is a proud Oakland native.

Helen Kupp

Helen is the Senior Director of Product Strategy & Partnerships of Future Forum, where she leads membership program development, and strategic partnerships. Previously, Helen led the Strategy & Analytics team at Slack, where she drove various cross-functional initiatives such as international launch and strategy, building our professional services offering, and leading Slack's fundraising and direct listing efforts.

Before Slack, Helen held various bizops and product roles at Thumbtack and BloomReach, primarily focused on launching and scaling new programs and functions. Prior to a career in technology, Helen was a consultant with Bain & Company.

Helen received a BS from Caltech and an MBA from Harvard Business School. She's a self-proclaimed introvert and a mom to a spunky toddler and a baby girl. Her playbooks are published on FutureForum.com, and she's passionate about advocating for and creating better support for working moms and caregivers.

Notes

Introduction

1. The Startups Team (2018). 'Slacking Off: Interview with Stewart Butterfield', Startups.com. Available at: https://www.startups.com/library/founder-stories/stewart-butterfield (Accessed: 18 November 2021).
2. Curran, E. (2021). 'Goldman says pandemic is shaping a more productive US economy', *Bloomberg*, 12 July. Available at: https://www.bloomberg.com/news/articles/2021-07-13/goldman-says-pandemic-is-shaping-a-more-productive-u-s-economy?srnd=future-of-work&sref=qysce8Zq (Accessed: 21 November 2021).
3. Deloitte (2021). '2021 Fortune/Deloitte CEO Survey', https://www2.deloitte.com/us/en/pages/chief-executive-officer/articles/ceo-survey.html (Accessed: 21 November 2021).
4. Subramanian, S. (2020). 'Farewell to the office?', *Future Forum*. 19 November. Available at: https://futureforum.com/2020/11/19/is-it-time-to-say-farewell-to-the-office/ (Accessed: 18 November 2021).
5. Thompson, D. (2014). 'A formula for perfect productivity: Work for 52 minutes, break for 17', *The Atlantic*, 17 September. Available at: https://www.theatlantic.com/business/archive/2014/09/science-tells-you-how-many-minutes-should-you-take-a-break-for-work-17/380369/ (Accessed: 18 November 2021).
6. Jacobson, L. (2015). 'Unions did not create the eight-hour work day and the 40-hour week. Henry Ford did', *Politifact*, 9 September. Available at: https://www.politifact.com/factchecks/2015/sep/09/viral-image/does-8-hour-day-and-40-hour-come-henry-ford-or-lab (Accessed: 19 November 2021).
7. Suzman, J. (2021). *Work: A deep history from the stone age to the age of robots*. New York: Penguin Publishing Group.

8. Cianciolo, B. and Vasel, K. (2021). 'The pandemic changed the way we work. 15 CEOs weigh in on what's next', *CNN Business*, 9 September. Available at: https://www.cnn.com/interactive/2021/09/business/perspectives/future-of-work-pandemic/index.html (Accessed: 19 November 2021).
9. Cianciolo, B. and Vasel, K. (2021). 'The pandemic changed the way we work. 15 CEOs weigh in on what's next', *CNN Business,* 9 September. Available at: https://www.cnn.com/interactive/2021/09/business/perspectives/future-of-work-pandemic/index.html (Accessed: 19 November 2021).

Chapter 1

1. Jones, S. (2021). 'Dropbox's billionaire founder Drew Houston says the 40-hour office week is a thing of the past and the pandemic has changed work', *Business Insider*, 28 September. Available at: https://www.businessinsider.com/dropbox-drew-houston-40-hour-office-work-week-is-over-2021-9 (Accessed: 18 November 2021).
2. Future Forum (2021). 'Future Forum pulse', October 2021. Available at: https://futureforum.com/pulse-survey/ (Accessed: 18 November 2021).
3. Deloitte (2021). '2021 Fortune/Deloitte CEO Survey'. Available at: https://www2.deloitte.com/us/en/pages/chief-executive-officer/articles/ceo-survey.html (Accessed: 18 November 2021).
4. Future Forum (2021). 'Winning the war for talent in the post-pandemic world', 15 June. Available at: https://futureforum.com/2021/06/15/future-forum-pulse/ (Accessed: 18 November 2021).
5. Fuller, J. B. and Raman, M. 'The caring company: How employers can cut costs and boost productivity by helping employees manage caregiving needs'. Available at: https://www.hbs.edu/managing-the-future-of-work/research/Pages/the-caring-company.aspx (Accessed: 18 November 2021).
6. Future Forum (2021). 'Winning the war for talent in the post-pandemic world', 15 June. Available at: https://futureforum.com/2021/06/15/future-forum-pulse/ (Accessed: 18 November 2021).
7. Bersin, J. (2013). 'Employee retention now a big issue: Why the tide has turned', *LinkedIn*, 16 August. Available at: https://www.linkedin.com/pulse/20130816200159-131079-employee-retention-now-a-big-issue-why-the-tide-has-turned/ (Accessed: 18 November 2021).
8. Gandhi, V. and Robison, J. (2021). 'The "Great Resignation" is really the "Great Discontent"', *Gallup,* 22 July. Available at: https://www.gallup.com/workplace/351545/great-resignation-really-great-discontent.aspx (Accessed: 18 November 2021).

9. Harter, J. (2021). 'U.S. employee engagement rises following wild 2020', *Gallup*, 26 February. Available at: https://www.gallup.com/workplace/330017/employee-engagement-rises-following-wild-2020.aspx (Accessed: 18 November 2021).

10. Chamorro-Premuzic, T. (2015). 'Why group brainstorming is a waste of time', *Harvard Business Review*, 25 March. Available at: https://hbr.org/2015/03/why-group-brainstorming-is-a-waste-of-time (Accessed: 18 November 2021).

11. Future Forum (2021). 'Winning the war for talent in the post-pandemic world', 15 June. Available at: https://futureforum.com/2021/06/15/future-forum-pulse/ (Accessed: 18 November 2021).

12. Choudhury, P. (R.) (2021). 'Our work-from-anywhere future', *Harvard Business Review*, November–December. Available at: https://hbr.org/2020/11/our-work-from-anywhere-future (Accessed: 18 November 2021).

13. Lorenzo, R., Voigt, N., Tsusaka, M. and Krentz, M. (2018). 'How diverse leadership teams boost innovation', 23 January. Available at: https://www.bcg.com/en-us/publications/2018/how-diverse-leadership-teams-boost-innovation (Accessed: 11 January 2022).

14. JoshBersin.com (2015). 'Why diversity and inclusion has become a business priority', 7 December. Available at: https://joshbersin.com/2015/12/why-diversity-and-inclusion-will-be-a-top-priority-for-2016/ (Accessed: 18 November 2021).

15. McKinsey & Company (2021). 'Race in the workplace: The black experience in the U.S. private sector', 21 February. Available at: https://www.mckinsey.com/featured-insights/diversity-and-inclusion/race-in-the-workplace-the-black-experience-in-the-us-private-sector (Accessed: 18 November 2021).

16. Subramanian, S. (2021). 'Moving from retrofit to redesign on diversity, equity, and inclusion: A how-to guide for leaders', *Future Forum*, 15 June. Available at: https://futureforum.com/2021/06/15/moving-from-retrofit-to-redesign/ (Accessed: 18 November 2021).

17. Subramanian, S. (2021). 'Moving from retrofit to redesign on diversity, equity, and inclusion: A how-to guide for leaders', *Future Forum*, 15 June. Available at: https://futureforum.com/2021/06/15/moving-from-retrofit-to-redesign/ (Accessed: 18 November 2021).

18. William Samuelson, W. (1988). 'Status quo bias in decision making', *Journal of Risk and Uncertainty*, 1, pp. 7–59 Available at: https://web.mit.edu/curhan/www/docs/Articles/biases/1_J_Risk_Uncertainty_7_(Samuelson).pdf (Accessed: 18 November 2021).

Step 1

1. Keller, V. (2015). 'The business case for purpose', *Harvard Business Review*. Available at: https://assets.ey.com/content/dam/ey-sites/ey-com/en_gl/topics/digital/ey-the-business-case-for-purpose.pdf (Accessed: 18 November 2021).
2. Pendleton, D. (2021). 'CEO who built GitLab fully remote worth $2.8 billion on IPO', *Bloomberg*, 14 October. Available at: https://www.msn.com/en-us/money/companies/ceo-who-built-gitlab-fully-remote-worth-2-6-billion-with-ipo/ar-AAPw2db (Accessed: 18 November 2021).
3. Sarasohn, E. (2021). 'The great executive-employee disconnect', *Future Forum*, 5 October. Available at: https://futureforum.com/2021/10/05/the-great-executive-employee-disconnect/ (Accessed: 18 November 2021).

Step 2

1. Cohen, J. R. and Single, L. E. (2001). 'An examination of the perceived impact of flexible work arrangements on professional opportunities in public accounting', *Journal of Business Ethics*. Available at: https://doi.org/10.1023/A:1010767521662 (Accessed: 30 November 2021).
2. Barrero, J. M., Bloom, N. and Davis, S. J. (2021). 'Don't force people to come back to the office full time', *Harvard Business Review*, 24 August. Available at: https://hbr.org/2021/08/I-force-people-to-come-back-to-the-office-full-time (Accessed: 18 November 2021).
3. Telstra 'Our leadership team'. Available at: https://www.telstra.com.au/aboutus/our-company/present/leadership-team (Accessed: 18 November 2021).
4. Jones, S. (2021). 'Slack is telling execs to limit their office days to 3 a week to encourage other staff to work from home', *Business Insider*, 29 September. Available at: https://www.businessinsider.com/slack-executives-come-into-office-less-set-remote-work-example-2021-9 (Accessed: 18 November 2021).
5. Sarasohn, E. (2021). 'The great executive-employee disconnect', *Future Forum*, 5 October. Available at: https://futureforum.com/2021/10/05/the-great-executive-employee-disconnect/ (Accessed: 18 November 2021).
6. Parker, P. (2020). *The Art of Gathering: How We Meet and Why It Matters*. New York: Penguin Publishing Group.
7. Perlow, L. A., Hadley, C. N. and Eun, E. (2017). 'Stop the meeting madness', *Harvard Business Review*, July–August. Available at: https://hbr.org/2017/07/stop-the-meeting-madness (Accessed: 18 November 2021).

8. Chamorro-Premuzic, T. (2015). 'Why group brainstorming is a waste of time', *Harvard Business Review*, 25 March. Available at: https://hbr. org/2015/03/why-group-brainstorming-is-a-waste-of-time (Accessed: 21 November 2021).

9. Mullen, B., Johnson, C. and Salas, E. (1991). 'Productivity loss in brain-storming groups: A meta-analytic integration', *Basic and Applied Social Psychology*, 12. Available at: https://www.tandfonline.com/doi/abs/10.1207/s15324834basp1201_1?journalCode=hbas20 (Accessed: 21 November 2021).

10. Stanford VMware Women's Leadership Innovation Lab (2021). 'Fostering inclusive workplaces: The remote work revolution', 12 October.

Step 3

1. Schiffer, Z. (2021). 'Apple asks staff to return to office three days a week starting in early September', *The Verge*, 2 June. Available at: https://www. theverge.com/2021/6/2/22465846/apple-employees-return-office-three-days-week-september (Accessed: 18 November 2021).

2. Schiffer, Z. (2021). 'Apple employees push back against returning to the office in internal letter', *The Verge*, 4 June. Available at: https://www. theverge.com/2021/6/4/22491629/apple-employees-push-back-return-office-internal-letter-tim-cook (Accessed: 18 November 2021).

3. Amazon.com (2021). 'Amazon offering teams more flexibility as we return to office', 11 October. Available at: https://www.aboutamazon.com/news/workplace/amazon-offering-teams-more-flexibility-as-we-return-to-office (Accessed: 18 November 2021).

4. Kupp, H. (2021). 'The hybrid how-to: How leaders can embrace flexible working models', *Future Forum*, 15 June. Available at: https://futureforum. com/2021/06/15/the-hybrid-how-to/ (Accessed: 18 November 2021).

5. Riedl, C. and Williams Woolley, A. (2020). 'Successful remote teams com-municate in bursts', *Harvard Business Review*, 28 October. Available at: https://hbr.org/2020/10/successful-remote-teams-communicate-in-bursts (Accessed: 18 November 2021).

6. Perlow, L. A., Hadley, C. A. and Eun, E. (2017). 'Stop the meeting madness', *Harvard Business Review*, July–August. https://hbr.org/2017/07/stop-the-meeting-madness (Accessed: 18 November 2021).

7. Ramachandran, V. (2021). 'Stanford researchers identify four causes for "Zoom fatigue" and their simple fixes', *Stanford News*, 23 February. Available at: https://news.stanford.edu/2021/02/23/four-causes-zoom-fatigue-solutions/ (Accessed: 18 November 2021).

Step 4

1. Dam, R. F. and Siang, T. Y. '5 stages in the design thinking process', *Interaction Design Foundation*. Available at: https://www.interaction-design.org/literature/article/5-stages-in-the-design-thinking-process (Accessed: 18 November 2021).
2. Duck, J. D. (1993). 'Managing change: The art of balancing', *Harvard Business Review*, November–December 1993. Available at: https://hbr.org/1993/11/managing-change-the-art-of-balancing (Accessed: 19 November 2021).
3. Duck, J. D. (1993). 'Managing change: The art of balancing', *Harvard Business Review*, November–December 1993. Available at: https://hbr.org/1993/11/managing-change-the-art-of-balancing (Accessed: 19 November 2021).

Step 5

1. Dr. Lieberman, M. and Dr. Eisenberger, N. (2008). 'The pains and pleasures of social life: a social cognitive neuroscience approach', *NeuroLeadership Journal*. Available at: https://www.scn.ucla.edu/pdf/Pains&Pleasures(2008).pdf (Accessed: 21 November 2021).
2. Deci, E. L. and Ryan R. M. (2014). 'Autonomy and need satisfaction in close relationships: Relationships motivation theory'. In N. Weinstein (Ed.), *Human Motivation and Interpersonal Relationships: Theory, Research, and Applications*. Springer Science + Business Media. https://doi.org/10.1007/978-94-017-8542-6_3 (Accessed: 21 November 2021).
3. HermanMiller.com. 'Belonging at work'. Available at: https://www.hermanmiller.com/research/categories/white-papers/belonging-at-work/ (Accessed: 20 November 2021).
4. Sarasohn, E. (2021). 'Priya Parker on what leaders should consider before bringing teams back together', *Future Forum*, 13 October. Available at: https://futureforum.com/2021/10/13/priya-parker-on-bringing-your-team-back-together/ (Accessed: 21 November 2021).
5. Statista (2020). 'Volume of commercial real estate transactions completed in the United States from 2007 to 2020', 24 June. Available at: https://www.statista.com/statistics/245103/real-estate-capital-flows/ (Accessed: 21 November 2021).
6. Shankman, S. (2020). '5 questions with GitLab's head of remote on business travel', *TripActions*, 19 June. Available at: https://tripactions.com/blog/q-and-a-darren-murph-head-of-remote-at-gitlab (Accessed: 21 November 2021).

7. Foster, W. (2019). 'How to run a company retreat for a remote team', Zapier, 1 April. Available at: https://zapier.com/learn/remote-work/how-run-company-retreat-remote-team/ (Accessed: 21 November 2021).
8. Foster, W. (2020). 'How to build culture in a remote team', Zapier, 18 March. Available at: https://zapier.com/learn/remote-work/how-build-culture-remote-team/ (Accessed: 21 November 2021).
9. Tippin, M., Kalbach, J. and Chin, D. (2018). 'The definitive guide to facilitating remote workshops', First edition, MURAL, June. Available at: https://assets.website-files.com/5ddd9c3f2186308353fe682d/5ea880b8d87d1751adea578b_The%20Definitive%20Guide%20To%20Facilitating%20Remote%20Workshops%20(V1.5).pdf (Accessed: 5 November 2021).
10. Macnee, D. (2021). 'Building a connected organization', Future Forum, 15 June. Available at: https://futureforum.com/2021/06/15/building-a-connected-organization/ (Accessed: 29 October 2021).
11. Macnee, D. (2021). 'Building a connected organization', Future Forum, 15 June. Available at: https://futureforum.com/2021/06/15/building-a-connected-organization/ (Accessed: 30 October 2021).
12. Work Life with Adam Grant (2021). 'Taken for granted: Indra Nooyi wants us to Reimagine the return to the office', 26 October.

Step 6

1. Bariso, J. (2018). 'Google spent a decade researching what makes a great boss. It came up with these 10 things', Inc., 18 July. Available at: https://www.inc.com/justin-bariso/google-spent-a-decade-researching-what-makes-a-great-boss-they-came-up-with-these-10-things.html (Accessed: 24 October 2021).
2. Milner, J. and Milner, T. (2018). 'Most managers don't know how to coach people. But they can learn', Harvard Business Review, 18 August. Available at: https://hbr.org/2018/08/most-managers-don't-know-how-to-coach-people-but-they-can-learn (Accessed: 5 November 2021).
3. Edelman. 'Edelman trust barometer 2021'. Available at: https://www.edelman.com/sites/g/files/aatuss191/files/2021-05/2021%20Edelman%20Trust%20Barometer%20Spring%20Update_0.pdf (Accessed: 19 November 2021).
4. Beck, R. and Harter, J. (2015). 'Managers account for 70% of variance in employee engagement', Gallup Business Journal, 21 April. Available at: https://news.gallup.com/businessjournal/182792/managers-account-variance-employee-engagement.aspx (Accessed: 25 October 2021).

5. Fayol, H. (2013). *General and Industrial Management*. Mansfield Centre, CT: Martino Fine Books.

6. Charterworks.com (2021). 'Interview: Why the best managers ask more questions', 3 October. Available at: https://www.charterworks.com/why-the-best-managers-ask-more-questions/ (Accessed: 25 October 2021).

7. Edmondson, A. C. (2018). *The fearless organization: Creating psychological safety in the workplace for learning, innovation, and growth.* Hoboken, NJ: Wiley.

8. McKinsey & Company (2021). 'Psychological safety and the critical role of leadership development', 11 February. Available at: https://www.mckinsey.com/business-functions/people-and-organizational-performance/our-insights/psychological-safety-and-the-critical-role-of-leadership-development (Accessed: 19 October 2021).

9. Grant, A. (2021). 'Building a culture of learning at work', *Strategy + Business*, 3 February. Available at: https://www.strategy-business.com/article/Building-a-culture-of-learning-at-work (Accessed: 23 October 2021).

10. Atkins, A. (2020). 'A modern leader's guide to organizational transparency', *Slack*, 1 October. Available at: https://slack.com/blog/transformation/a-modern-leaders-guide-to-organizational-transparency (Accessed: 19 October 2021).

11. Kossek, E. E., Barber, A. E. and Winters, D. (1999). 'Using flexible schedules in the managerial world: The power of peers', *Human Resource Management*, 8 March. Available at: https://onlinelibrary.wiley.com/doi/abs/10.1002/(SICI)1099-050X(199921)38:1%3C33::AID-HRM4%3E3.0.CO;2-H (Accessed: 25 October 2021).

12. McGregor, L. and Doshi, N. (2015). 'How company culture shapes employee motivation', *Harvard Business Review*, 25 November. Available at: https://hbr.org/2015/11/how-company-culture-shapes-employee-motivation?registration=success&registration=success (Accessed: 24 October 2021).

13. Blackwell, A. G. (2017). 'The curb-cut effect', *Stanford Social Innovation Review*, Winter. Available at: https://ssir.org/articles/entry/the_curb_cut_effect (Accessed: 24 October 2021).

14. Blackwell, A. G. (2020). 'Why the curb-cut effect is key to beating COVID-19', *PolicyLink*, 12, 1 July. Available at: https://www.policylink.org/commentary/curb-cut (Accessed: 24 October 2021).

15. Cross, R., Benson, M., Kostal, J. and Milnor, M. J. (2021). 'Collaboration overload is sinking productivity', *Harvard Business Review*, 7 September. Available at: https://hbr.org/2021/09/collaboration-overload-is-sinking-productivity (Accessed: 24 October 2021).

16. Stanford VMware Women's Leadership Innovation Lab (2021). 'Fostering inclusive workplaces: The remote work revolution', 12 October.

Step 7

1. Mortensen, M. and Gardner, H. K. (2021). 'WFH is corroding our trust in each other', *Harvard Business Review*, 10 February. Available at: https://hbr.org/2021/02/wfh-is-corroding-our-trust-in-each-other (Accessed: 20 October 2021).

2. Mortensen, M. and Gardner, H. K. (2021). 'WFH is corroding our trust in each other', *Harvard Business Review*, 10 February. Available at: https://hbr.org/2021/02/wfh-is-corroding-our-trust-in-each-other (Accessed: 20 October 2021).

3. Price, D. (2021). 'It's time to stop measuring productivity', Work Life, *Atlassian*, 10 August. Available at: https://www.atlassian.com/blog/productivity/the-problem-with-productivity-metrics (Accessed:21 October 2021).

4. Kantor, B. (2018). 'The RACI matrix: Your blueprint for project success', *CIO*, 30 January. Available at: https://www.cio.com/article/2395825/project-management-how-to-design-a-successful-raci-project-plan.html (Accessed: 27 October 2021).

5. Gallup (2020). 'State of the American workplace report', 6 February. Available at: https://www.gallup.com/workplace/285818/state-american-workplace-report.aspx (Accessed: 26 October 2021).

6. Gallup (2017). 'State of the American workplace report'. Available at: https://qualityincentivecompany.com/wp-content/uploads/2017/02/SOAW-2017.pdf (Accessed: 20 October 2021).

7. Morgan, B. (2018). 'The un-ignorable link between employee experience and customer experience', *Forbes*, 23 February. Available at: https://www.forbes.com/sites/blakemorgan/2018/02/23/the-un-ignorable-link-between-employee-experience-and-customer-experience/?sh=36a349b848dc (Accessed: 20 October 2021).

8. Judd, S., O'Rourke, E. and Grant, A. (2018). 'Employee surveys are still one of the best ways to measure engagement', *Harvard Business Review*, 14 March. Available at: https://hbr.org/2018/03/employee-surveys-are-still-one-of-the-best-ways-to-measure-engagement (Accessed: 27 October 2021).

Resources

1. Eliza Sarasohn, "Priya Parker on What Leaders Should Consider Before Bringing Teams Back Together," Future Forum, October 13, 2021, https://futureforum.com/2021/10/13/priya-parker-on-bringing-your-team-back-together/.

Index

Page numbers followed by *f* refer to figures.

223